The Washington Papers/112   Volume XII

CHINA'S FOREIGN POLICY TOWARD THE THIRD WORLD

·LILLIAN CRAIG HARRIS

Foreword by Harry Harding

Published with The Center for
Strategic and International Studies,
Georgetown University, Washington, D.C.

PRAEGER

New York
Westport, Connecticut
London

T0353536

Library of Congress Cataloging in Publication Data

Harris, Lillian Craig.
  China's foreign policy toward the Third World.

  (The Washington papers, ISSN 0278-937X; vol. XII,
112)
  Bibliography: p.
  1. Developing countries–Foreign relations–China.
  2. China–Foreign relations–Developing countries.
  I. Title.
  D888.C6H37   1984   327.510172′4   84-23744
  ISBN 0-275-91649-9

The views expressed in this paper are those of the author and do not necessarily reflect either official U.S. policy or the position of the Department of
State.

The *Washington Papers* are written under the auspices of The Center
for Strategic and International Studies (CSIS), Georgetown University,
and published with CSIS by Praeger Publishers. The views expressed in these
papers are those of the authors and not necessarily those of The Center.

Copyright © 1985 by The Center for Strategic and International Studies

All rights reserved. No portion of this book may be
reproduced, by any process or technique, without the
express written consent of the publisher.

Library of Congress Catalog Card Number: 84-23744
ISBN: 0-275-91649-9

First published in 1985

Praeger Publishers, 521 Fifth Avenue, New York, NY 10175
A division of Greenwood Press, Inc.

Printed in the United States of America

The paper used in this book complies with the Permanent
Paper Standard issued by the National Information Standards
Organization (Z39.48-1984).

10 9 8 7 6 5 4 3 2

Contents

Foreword

Although Beijing's relations with the Third World are a central element in Chinese foreign policy, they have received surprisingly little detailed scholarly attention. Admittedly, most compendia on China's foreign relations usually contain a chapter or two on Beijing's policy toward the developing countries. But this paper by Lillian Craig Harris is the first full-length treatment of the subject since the publication in 1970 of Peter Van Ness's pathbreaking study, *Revolution and Chinese Foreign Policy*. Harris's concise and lucid overviews of China's current relations with particular countries and regions in the developing world, in chapter 4, and of Beijing's policies on major international economic and political issues, in chapter 5, will be of particular value to readers interested in the politics of the Third World or in contemporary Chinese foreign policy.

Moreover, much has changed in China's relations with the Third World during the 15 years between the appearance of Van Ness's book and the completion of Harris's present work. In the late 1960s, during the Cultural Revolution, Chinese policy toward the developing countries embodied Beijing's total rejection of the international system dominated by the United States and the Soviet Union. In those years, China maintained friendly relations with only a few Third World governments; offered rhetorical support, and some material assistance, to a large number of revolutionary movements in Asia, Africa, and Latin America; and sought to limit the extension of both Soviet and U.S. influence throughout the developing world.

By the late 1970s, in contrast, Chinese foreign policy had come to reflect a very different concern. As China became aware of the military expansion of the Soviet Union and the direct threat that it posed to Chinese security, Beijing's relations with the Third World, so revolutionary in tone in the previous decade, took on a much more conservative character. China greatly attenuated – even if it did not completely break – its relations with national liberation movements and revolutionary Communist parties and established or expanded normal state-to-state ties with a wide range of Third World governments. It virtually ceased its calls for a reordering of the international economic system and sought instead to forge a "united front" of both the developed and the developing worlds against Soviet hegemonism. It announced its opposition to virtually every Soviet initiative in the Third World and began to support – sometimes tacitly, but frequently openly – almost all U.S. policies in Asia, Africa, and the Middle East.

By the early 1980s, Chinese foreign policy had changed once again, although in a more subtle and less dramatic manner. For reasons of both domestic politics and strategic advantage, China undertook to replace its image as a quasi-ally of the United States with a more "independent" foreign policy and sought to turn from confrontation to reconciliation in its relations with the Soviet Union. While continuing to voice concern about the expansion of Soviet influence, particularly in Asia, China adopted a somewhat more evenhanded approach to the two superpowers' policy in the Third World, criticizing U.S. policy in Central America and the Middle East as well as Soviet initiatives in Southeast and Southwest Asia. And, while opening its door to trade and investment with the West, Beijing revived its earlier support for the creation of a new international economic order.

In this monograph, Lillian Harris provides a useful account of these twists and turns, as she traces the evolution of China's policy toward the Third World from 1949 to the present. But she also correctly emphasizes that behind these changes in China's posture toward the developing countries lie some significant continuities. Consistently since 1949, China has identified itself with the Third World, portraying itself a developing country that shares both historical experiences and contemporary interests with the states of Asia, Africa, and Latin America. Equally consistently, Beijing has insisted that the growing influence of the Third World is the most important feature of postwar international politics and is one that will ultimately doom the attempts of the two superpowers to establish global hegemony. As a result, Beijing has also repeatedly calculated that the Third World was a useful arena for promoting its national security, winning international recognition, and displaying its commitment to progressive principles in international affairs.

Looking ahead, Dr. Harris raises two critical issues in China's future relations with the Third World: the degree to which Beijing will continue to cast its lot with the developing countries and the extent to which China will be able to expand its influence in the capitals of Asia, Africa, and Latin America.

On the first point—the salience of the Third World to China—Dr. Harris notes the existence of somewhat contradictory trends. To the extent that the Third World was a vehicle by which Beijing could achieve international legitimacy and recognition after 1949 – a status that the United States attempted to deny to the People's Republic until the early 1970s – it has largely served its purpose. China has now won universal acceptance as a major power in Asia and is increasingly regarded as an emergent world power as well. In some ways, in other words, China has graduated from the Third World and has entered the ranks of the major powers. As a result, some Chinese policy analysts have begun to suggest that the Third World should receive less attention in Chinese foreign affairs and that Beijing should place greatest emphasis on managing its relations with the two superpowers and with Japan.

And yet this viewpoint appears thus far to reflect a minority opinion in Beijing. The Third World continues to play a major substantive and symbolic role in Chinese foreign policy. Substantively, Beijing sees much to be gained through economic interaction with Third World countries and through support for Third World demands for a reform of the international economic order. It still regards the developing countries as the focal point in the global competition between Moscow and Washington and the area in which Soviet (and, occasionally, U.S.) expansion must be resisted. Symbolically, too, Third World issues provide a convenient opportunity for China to demonstrate its independence from the two superpowers and its continuing commitment to a progressive foreign policy.

Nonetheless, the element of ambivalence in Chinese foreign policy toward the Third World that is evident today is likely to persist in the years ahead, as China tries to balance its ties with the developed world with its relations with Asia, Africa, and Latin America. This ambivalence reflects the fact that, alone in the world, China is simultaneously a developing country and a major power. Beijing rules a nation that, in Harris's words, is "an emerging power with global responsibility, but one that still desires to portray itself as a member of the developing world."

The second issue concerns the opposite question: the salience of China to the Third World and the influence that Beijing is likely to enjoy over Third World governments in the coming years. Here, Dr. Harris presents a complex balance sheet. On the one hand, China's size and resources, its skill at international diplomacy, and its description of itself as a developing country all give it substantial influence in Third World capitals. On the other hand, China's emergence as a major power is already breeding some apprehension, particularly in the rest of Asia, about Beijing's longer-term capabilities and intentions; and its growing involvement in international economic affairs may make it a competitor with other developing countries for markets and capital.

What is more, as Dr. Harris acknowledges, China has remained somewhat aloof from close cooperation with the Third World on a number of issues of central concern and has steadfastly refused to join such Third World organizations as the Group of 77 and the Non-Aligned Movement. This, too, raises suspicions that Beijing is more concerned with its own strategic and economic advantage than with the collective interests of the developing world as a whole.

In short, one can legitimately question whether China will, in fact, acquire the active leadership role in the Third World that Harris predicts for it, or even whether Beijing will seek such a role. Thus far, China has few close allies in the Third World and disclaims any desire to find any. Its relations with a number of important Third World countries, including India, Indonesia, Vietnam, and Cuba, are either hostile or strained. It has been more a cheerleader than an active participant in the movement to reform the international economic system. And, outside Southeast Asia, it has undertaken few successful attempts to restrict the expansion of superpower influence. Thus, it may be more realistic to conclude that Chinese influence in the Third World will remain limited and that China, as in the past, will be better able to maintain friendly bilateral relations with a wide range of developing states than to influence their policies on issues involving third countries or multilateral problems.

What are the implications of this analysis for the United States? If the late 1970s suggested that we need no longer fear inevitable Chinese opposition to U.S. initiatives in the Third World, the early 1980s warned us that we cannot expect automatic Chinese support. In fact, perhaps the most specific consequence of China's "independent" foreign policy is that Beijing will reach decisions on issues involving the Third World on a case-by-case basis. Thus, Beijing and Washington are likely to find common ground on some issues, particularly those featuring direct expansion in the Third World by the Soviet Union and its proxies, but may well discover differences on other matters, such as international economic reform, arms control and disarmament, and instances of conflict and instability in which Soviet involvement is less apparent. Fortunately for the United States, the areas of agreement between the two countries tend to be those of greatest importance to China, such as the security of Asia, while the areas of difference are of somewhat lesser importance to Beijing.

China's influence in the Third World will continue to be modest for some time to come. Whether it chooses to cast its weight on the side of the United States or against it, outside of Asia China is unlikely to be the decisive factor in shaping the outcome of major issues involving the Third World. Nonetheless, as China engages more actively in global diplomacy and as the resources at its disposal steadily grow, Beijing's influence on international issues should also increase. Accordingly, an understanding of Chinese policy toward the Third World, such as that which Lillian Craig Harris shares with us here, will be of considerable significance to all those interested in contemporary international affairs.

Harry Harding
Senior Fellow
Foreign Policy Studies Program
The Brookings Institution

October 1984

About the Author

Lillian Craig Harris is a foreign service officer who worked as a journalist, a teacher, and a UN public information officer before joining the Department of State in 1976. Currently the political analyst for Egypt and Libya in the Department's Bureau of Intelligence and Research, she has also served in that bureau as a political analyst on China and on Afghanistan. She has a master's degree in modern Middle East history from the American University of Beirut and a doctorate in Asian history from Georgetown University. Dr. Harris frequently lectures and publishes on China's foreign relations and recently returned from several months of advanced Mandarin training in Taiwan. She is the daughter and granddaughter of missionaries to China and is married to Alan Goulty, a British diplomat.

1

Determinants of Chinese Foreign Policy

In a recent public statement, former Chinese Ambassador to the United States Chai Zemin said that "The American people long to understand China." Although this assessment may be somewhat optimistic – the American people, like the Chinese people, are for the most part preoccupied domestically and moved primarily by those issues that directly influence their daily lives – there is a growing awareness in the United States of China's importance throughout the world. China's increasing leadership role in the Third World is one such area of importance.

Since 1949, China's attitudes toward the Third World have significantly shaped China's foreign policy. Beijing's attempt to adopt an "independent" foreign policy, as outlined at the twelfth party congress in September 1982, continues to reflect this. Although relations with the Third World are not the major ingredient in China's foreign policy – that position is reserved for domestic political considerations – the Third World relationship is important to the People's Republic of China (PRC) as a counterbalance to the superpowers, as a sphere for China's influence elsewhere, and as a symbol of China's independence.

1

Beijing's claim to an independent foreign policy is primarily intended to stress China's nonreliance on the superpowers. But independence is not equidistance. Chinese leaders have pointed out that the PRC intends to continue to tilt more toward the United States than toward the USSR. Despite Beijing's professional membership in the Third World, for economic and security reasons interaction with the United States clearly has higher priority for China. Moreover, the PRC's foreign policy remains quite reactive to the policies of both superpowers and is therefore not truly independent. Although Beijing's efforts to influence the Third World and to gain prominence as its spokesman grow logically from China's fundamental national concerns and historical experience, the direction and tone of China's ties with Third World states have been and continue to be colored by Beijing's relationship with both Washington and Moscow.

Despite certain intrinsic difficulties, which have always limited China in its ability to influence the Third World or to use it as a political platform, in the 1960s China, according to China scholar Peter Van Ness, "apparently saw the Third World as the area of greatest political opportunity on the contemporary world scene. It was a world in flux, one in which old political orders and alliances were crumbling and new ones were being formed – an area where new friends could be won, old balances of power upset, and powerful new alliances established."[1] Despite the passage of a quarter of a century, this perception and opportunity are still true.

China's foreign policy is not, moreover, one of specific alignment with the Third World. Although Beijing seeks to identify itself publicly with the Third World, it asserts its right to act quite independently and even at times to maintain an aloofness from issues at the working level – as illustrated by China's relative passivity in certain international organizations and especially by its failure to join various Third World groups. This aloofness has roots in Chinese history and can be attributed to the not unreasonable desire to stand apart from international divisions and retain the ability to manipulate events to China's advantage. There is, nonetheless, some question of the extent to which the PRC does in reality regard itself as a Third World country and even about whether China is truly a member of this Third World.

Yet the desire for international prominence is related to the Chinese search for what every country wants: security, recognition, and, more recently, modernization. The PRC seeks national independence and reunification, a regional sphere of influence in Asia, a position as spokesman for the Third World and the nonaligned, and a recognition of China's rightful place as a world power – a nation whose influence and responsible actions show it to be of world class importance. Reflecting these goals, the *Beijing Review* recently described the three basic objectives of Chinese foreign policy as (1) opposition to hegemonism (i.e., independence), (2) the strengthening of unity and cooperation among Third World countries (i.e., recognition and leadership), and (3) the safeguarding of world peace (i.e., security and development).[2]

China's present foreign policy is related to Mao's famous "Theory of the Differentiation of the Three Worlds,"* particularly in the importance that theory attaches to the Third

---

*Basically, Mao divided the world into three spheres: the First World of the two superpowers, the United States and the USSR; the Second World essentially comprising the developed world of Europe and Japan; and the Third World, whose membership includes both socialist countries and the oppressed, underdeveloped nations. Mao described the Third World as "the main force in the worldwide struggle against imperialism and hegemonism" and said that, although the Second World oppresses and exploits the Third, it is itself "controlled and bullied by the superpowers." This contradiction can be exploited by the Third World to win over the Second and unite with it in the common struggle for self-determination.

World and the advice it provides on how to manage the super-powers.[3] There have been few specific references, however, to the Three Worlds theory by Beijing in recent years, and particularly since 1982, Beijing's focus on the importance of the North-South dialogue and international negotiations and cooperation has considerably watered down the theory's application of class struggle to international conflict. In fact, a new doctrinal foundation for Chinese foreign policy seems now to be emerging, which could supersede both the Three Worlds theory as well as the central Chinese doctrine of the united front against hegemonism, providing instead for a new Chinese independence, even from the Third World.

As the PRC government formally declared in 1982, China desires normal relations in so far as possible with all states, including the superpowers. By implication, this policy removes China from a position of unrelenting opposition to the superpowers – although Beijing has continued its severe public criticism of the policies of both Moscow and Washington. Because the new independent policy repudiates all alliances, there is also the implication that a close Chinese-Third World united front against the superpowers will ultimately no longer be desirable. Rhetorically, however, Beijing continues to call for Third World pressure against the developed world to equalize economic and political advantage and thus create greater international stability.

China nevertheless consistently denies that it aspires to leadership of the Third World and says it will never seek superpower status (a pejorative term in the PRC lexicon) or try to assert "hegemony" over other states. Yet Beijing's statements about the Third World frequently read like campaign speeches, demonstrating China's promotion of itself as guide to unity and cooperation in the developing world. What China actually seeks in the Third World is influence, not outright domination. To this end, China's leaders now see an unprecedented opportunity within an increasingly multipolar world.

For Beijing, the world situation offers both hope and danger. A New China News Agency (NCNA) commentator summarized 1983 as a year of "disturbing troubles, mounting tensions and actual conflicts sparked by the arms race, super-power rivalry in the Third World and a worsening North-South economic relationship . . . ," in which, nonetheless, "an ever more diversified world" has undercut superpower influence and brought opportunity for "growing strength and influence of the Third World." The commentary ends on a note of praise for Third World countries which "have come to see the dire need for unity and mutual assistance in their cause of independence and economic development." The objective, of course, is to suggest China's leadership in the endeavor.

How this will be worked out has yet to be demonstrated. But since its entry into the UN in 1971, a success made possible by Third World support, China has steadily increased its influence as a spokesman for the Third World. China already has considerably more influence in the developing world because of its size, cultural antiquity, history, and achievements than Westerners generally recognize—including its position as the only Third World country with a permanent seat on the UN Security Council. Many Third World states envy China's ability to rebuff or accept the wooing of the superpowers seemingly at will. At the same time, many developing countries regard China itself as a burgeoning superpower—but without a threatening military capability—with whom it might make sense to align and whose influence can be used to manipulate the real superpowers.

On the other hand, China's path to Third World authority is beset with obstacles, including concern among China's neighbors over Beijing's ultimate regional intentions and increasing Chinese competition with other Third World states for international markets and development funds. The Third World is, moreover, ever more difficult to define, including as it does oil-rich Arab states, African nations of Fourth World poverty, certain East European countries but not others (by

China's definition),* and several rapidly developing capitalist countries of Asia and Latin America. (A convenient central assumption of China's Third World policy is that, despite diversity, developing countries are still characterized by a unity of interests.)

A particular difficulty arises in regard to China's relations with its Third World neighbors. Although East Asia will be treated here in the context of China's Third World relationships, a word of caution is necessary. Regional security concerns and a historical tradition of China *primus inter pares* makes East Asia clearly special to Beijing and consequently presents a unique set of concerns and opportunities. Chinese policy in Asia thus cannot always be regarded as characteristic of Chinese policy in the Third World in general.

Many Third World countries, moreover, see China as spiritually alien. This is due as much to lack of knowledge about China as to China's failure to present itself as a nation of individuals rather than as a conformist, closed society. The post-Cultural Revolution's "opening" of China has not yet done away with an image problem that includes an ingredient of fear of Chinese reversion to radical behavior patterns. Finally, Third World states are aware of other differences between themselves and China, most notably the magnitude of its size

---

*China's definition of the Third World has fluctuated through the years. Placement of East European states in the Third World has depended on China's relationship with each and their political distance from Moscow. Thus, Albania, Romania, and Yugoslavia (after 1977) are defined by Beijing as socialist countries and part of the Third World. The PRC is apparently in the process of redefining the other Eastern bloc states from "social imperialist" to "socialist." References to the Third World in this study are in accord with the present Chinese definition: the term includes practically every nation except the superpowers, Japan, Western Europe, and the East European states dominated by Moscow.

and population, the legacy of a semi-colonial as opposed to a colonial history, and China's diversified resource base as opposed to the reliance of many Third World economies on one or two major resources.

Where then can Chinese efforts to achieve Third World leadership be effective and where and how can Beijing attempt to apply leverage? China's answer appears to lie partly in efforts to stimulate Third World awareness of the potential power of its collective influence and partly in emphasizing an issues-related approach. These are reflected in the PRC's increasing activity in Third World organizations, its championship of Third World issues such as nuclear disarmament and a new international economic order, and its espousal of Third World positions in regard to such issues as Law of the Sea and North-South negotiations.

In the foreseeable future Beijing's Third World policy will remain geared to keeping the superpowers off balance, or, in other words, seeking to benefit from superpower rivalry and playing on Third World perceptions of exploitation by the developed world. Persistent themes in the PRC's quest for influence in the Third World include opposition to political or economic domination by the superpowers and promotion of radical changes in the world economic order so that even the poorest nations can obtain their economic "rights."

In its self-appointed role as adviser-facilitator to the Third World, China could eventually seek formal allies, although proxies will probably continue to be the preferred method of influence. Chinese Communist Party (CCP) leader Hu Yaobang told a Yugoslav delegation in May 1984 that "China refrains from seeking alliance with any other countries including Third World countries." The Chinese historically have not entrusted themselves to alliances and would undoubtedly prefer to retain the position of "elder brother," whose word is trusted, whose advice is sought, and whose influence is solicited.

Legacy of History and Culture

The basic determinants of Chinese foreign policy have remained consistent, just as Beijing's basic modern goals of security, recognition, and modernization have never changed — although altered circumstances may have shifted the ordering of priorities. In the earliest period of PRC foreign policy the core ideas and concepts that by the mid-1970s would evolve into the Three Worlds theory were already evident. The legacy of China's past, the influence of internal politics on external, and the critical relationships to the United States and the USSR are the major determinants behind the process of constant reinterpretation.

The Chinese, with roots deep in the world's oldest continuous cultural tradition, are more likely than many other peoples to view political events as part of a broad historical spectrum. This propensity is reinforced for China's leaders by the Marxist philosophy of historical determinism. Self-conscious about China's historical uniqueness and armed with a doctrine that explains to their satisfaction both the failures and triumphs of ancient and modern history, China's current leaders tend to interpret all events against the background of Chinese history and in the context of China's perceived righteousness and betrayal by others.

China's concept of its historical centrality and its right to cultural preeminence is still a determining aspect of the Chinese world view. At the root of the efforts in recent years to exclude foreign cultures and ideas is the continuing influence of the concept of the superiority of "Chineseness," a belief that increases the difficulties Chinese face in understanding the political and cultural traditions of other societies, including those in the developing world. The historical legacy of the Confucian principle of China's universal authority continues to color political thinking in China despite the commitment of modern leadership to an ideology whose ultimate source lies outside China.

Modern history, in particular the past 150 years of exploitation by more economically developed countries, is yet another significant determinant of Beijing's international attitudes and actions. In concert with much of the rest of the Third World, modern China interprets history according to a framework that emphasizes the inroads of imperialism. There is as well a sense in which China's leaders believe the PRC deserves special treatment as retribution for past disservice. The PRC does not, however, reserve the philosophy of such retribution for itself alone. Its pronouncements are typically replete with references to the need for economic concessions and international readjustments to compensate for past exploitation of the underdeveloped world by colonialism and for the present inequities attributed to capitalism. Such philosophy lies at the heart of China's support for a new international economic order.

China's magnificent cultural and historical heritage has made the recent years of its weakness – even, at times, insignificance – an extremely bitter and frustrating experience for Chinese intellectuals and leaders. Acceptance of this condition, described by one scholar as "cultural despair," has had a profound impact on the country's foreign policy.[4] A recent example of Chinese touchiness on historical issues relating to national pride was displayed in Beijing's 1982 reaction to publication in Japan of textbooks that downplayed Japanese atrocities in China during the 1930s. The Chinese reaction – along with that of South Korea and other Asian Third World countries – was sufficiently shrill to cause the Japanese to revise the offending textbooks. In early 1983 Beijing reacted strongly once again to a perceived slight to China's position, this time involving allegations that U.S. Secretary of State George Shultz had described the PRC as a "regional power."

Under the influence of its historical legacy, the PRC finds itself in one sense modeling its Third World behavior on an idea that is practically as old as China itself. Under the tributary arrangements carried out for hundreds of years between China and its less influential neighbors, China's preeminence was recognized and homage paid. The tributary states received benefit of recognition and its attendant prestige and were allowed to conduct their affairs internally and among themselves quite independently as long as such activities did not impinge on China's own interests or sovereignty.

The persistence in the PRC of the Confucian tradition of China's supremacy combined with China's lack of experience in dealing with other nations as equals raises the question of whether what China seeks is not actually an old situation in new guise. The Southeast Asian nations fear that Beijing's enhanced international position makes a new "tributary" system less unrealistic than it may appear. Moreover, whether or not the idea is fantastic, it appears to hold great attraction for elements inside the Chinese leadership. China's anger over Vietnam's refusal to recognize Indochina as a historical sphere of Chinese influence is a clear example. It is arguable that Beijing would not have objected to a Vietnamese assertion of control over Indochina if Hanoi had not rejected Chinese for Soviet sponsorship and had underlined its recognition of the preeminence of China by consulting with Beijing.

Internal Political Dynamics

As has been illustrated many times over the past 30 years, China's domestic and foreign policies are inexorably linked, not the least in the way the PRC's internal economic experiences are mirrored in the economic advice and assistance provided by China abroad. For example, the failure in the late 1950s of internal economic policies that emphasized development of heavy industry and a consequent switch to emphasis on the importance of light industrial development was reflected in China's aid programs in Africa, where the PRC typically financed light industry projects. The open split with

Moscow in 1960 left China virtually bereft of external aid and saw a consequent upswing in Chinese rhetoric concerning the value of self-reliance.[5] A more recent example has been the policy of an "open door" to the West, motivated to a high degree by a desire to further China's internal modernization.

Foreign policy issues, such as relations with the superpowers and war with Vietnam, have been extremely important in the post-Mao Zedong succession struggle, as various factions have capitalized upon perceived policy failures. The post-Mao era is characterized by a switch in emphasis from politics to economics, and the PRC faces enormous problems in seeking to bury Mao's policies while praising Mao and in trying to avoid internal social turmoil and economic instability by not modernizing too rapidly or in ways inappropriate to China's unique conditions. Balancing its relations with the rest of the world while implementing modernization is a delicate task.

Powerful bureaucratic and institutional interests in China have criticized the policy of strengthening ties to the developed world, especially to the United States, to achieve domestic benefits. The failure of the leadership of Vice Premier Deng Xiaoping to achieve progress on the reintegration of Taiwan with the mainland has been used by domestic critics to resist institutional and political reforms at home. Criticism that China is becoming dependent upon the West has slowed progress in domestic reforms sought by Deng's supporters and is certainly related to the 1982 policy shift that brought Beijing to reemphasize its Third World credentials and proclaim an independent foreign policy.

For their part, the reformers (moderates) have used the economic failures and domestic turmoil of the Maoist past to discredit their political opponents and to encourage greater openness to the West. Domestic debate continues in the context of, or even as a vehicle for, debate of foreign policy. Traditionalists (radicals), who since the mid-1970s have opposed the emphasis of the Three Worlds theory on a united front with "non-revolutionary elements" and making of "hegemonism" rather than capitalism or imperialism the main enemy, have themselves been harshly criticized for failure in the 1960s of the policies – both foreign and domestic – advocated by their particularly Maoist package of solutions.

The mid-1982 Chinese move to emphasize its Third World credentials reflects the desire of a loose amalgam of Deng's critics to free China from the constraints and liabilities of perceived "dependence" on the United States. For this group, Third World leadership means a position of freestanding authority. By adopting a compromise position of opposition to both Soviet "hegemonistic" military expansion and U.S. "hegemonistic" economic interference, these Chinese leaders hope to gain greater international influence while defusing domestic disagreement.

Internal economic need is also a major determinant of China's foreign policy. Concentration on internal domestic need dramatically reduced Chinese aid programs to the Third World in the late 1970s. Revision of the long-held doctrine of self-reliance has, since the late 1970s, allowed China to accept loans from foreign institutions and foreign governments and has even led to Chinese laws allowing foreign ownership of and investment in commercial enterprises in China. Membership in the International Development Association (IDA) and the International Bank for Reconstruction and Development (the World Bank) and recent moves toward membership in the Asian Development Bank (ADB) illustrate this new flexibility based on domestic priorities.

But Chinese competition for available international development aid has serious and as yet unexplored implications for the PRC's relationships with the Third World. Moreover, the need for foreign exchange to fuel the modernization program has brought interesting changes in the PRC's arms supply policy to the Third World: Beijing has sold arms to selected Third World countries since 1979.

The 1983-1984 campaign against "spiritual pollution" from the West arose at least in part from the Chinese leadership's desire to prevent popular expectations for an improved standard of living from rising more rapidly than could realistically be met. Chinese failure to react against "spiritual pollution" originating in the Third World states reflects recognition of the relative weakness of Third World cultures in comparison to both China and the developed world. There are comparatively few Third World tourists, scholars, and businessmen in China and their life styles are not in any case likely to be emulated. Perhaps the single area that poses the possible threat of direct cultural "pollution" from the Third World is in the contacts between the Islamic world and China's more than 20 million Muslims.[6] Such contact is encouraged for political reasons but is strictly controlled and monitored by the Chinese Communist Party, whose officials frequently repeat the PRC's constitutional injunction against foreign control of religious life in China.

Finally, domestic events themselves are important in China's foreign relations in that they color foreign perceptions of China and help determine the extent of both external economic commitment and foreign diplomatic confidence. Beijing's efforts in recent years to formulate legal codes and move toward government by law rather than leadership fiat has inspired foreign confidence. But such events as the trial of the "Gang of Four," xenophobic attacks on African students in China, the party rectification drive, and antispiritual pollution activities have served to lower foreign confidence, including that of the Third World.

Primacy of the Moscow-Beijing-Washington Triangle

The past 30 years have seen considerable changes in China's description of the relative dangers posed to the world by the two superpowers. China's closest ally and its greatest enemy in 1950 had switched places by 1980. During the intervening 30 years, the positions of the two superpowers gradually equalized, and they were both described by Beijing in the 1960s as "colluding and contending." By the late 1970s, however, Moscow had achieved precedence as "the greatest threat to international peace." Beginning in 1981, both the United States and the Soviet Union were once again being termed sources of serious threat to international peace and stability, although the United States was usually presented more as bungling and misguided than evil.

Fluctuations in current definitions are likely to continue. What Beijing cannot afford, however, is hostility toward both superpowers at once. Such a policy was tried during the 1960s and served only to heighten China's international isolation and insecurity. Thus Beijing moves carefully in its current efforts to strike an independent pose.

Although Beijing has publicly excoriated the idea of a Sino-Soviet-U.S. triangular relationship – the tightening of any angle of which stretches the opposite sides – it is precisely this concept translated into geopolitical terms that, since 1949, has been the strongest external determinant of China's foreign policy. In July 1984, Huan Xiang, a respected Chinese political commentator, argued in print that international developments are determined by the "great triangular relations" between China, the United States, and the Soviet Union. Huan not only assigned China a position as a major power, but actually downplayed the importance of the Third World. Although his commentary may not reflect official Chinese doctrine, it probably does represent the belief of a significant group of prominent Chinese intellectuals who assign the Third World a lower rung of importance than does official PRC policy.

The tie-in between China's internal and external policies is dramatically illustrated by Beijing's relations with Washington and Moscow. The Chinese leadership has frequently used both Soviet and U.S. boogeymen to stimulate popular support or acceptance of internal policies. The "oppose America" campaign during the Korean conflict in the early 1950s was the first such example. In subsequent years, dramatization of the threat from the north or from the west has been used to mobilize the entire country to smelt iron, store grain, plant trees, and kill vermin.

In the 1960s, internal power struggles between the civilian and military leaders centered around whether or not to repair ties with Moscow and how far to cooperate with the Soviet Union in providing military aid to Vietnam. An important aspect of the power struggle that led to Defense Minister Lin Piao's attempted coup and subsequent death in 1971 was the debate over the budding Sino-U.S. détente. Evidence suggests that domestic controversy on the subject of Chinese ties to both Moscow and Washington has continued up to the present.

Deng Xiaoping's much celebrated early 1979 visit to the United States immediately following Sino-U.S. normalization of diplomatic relations is a persuasive example of the use by China of the "America card." Relations between China and Vietnam had deteriorated seriously in previous weeks and there was concern in Washington that China would destabilize Southeast Asia and risk large scale Soviet retaliation by seeking militarily to break up the growing Vietnamese relationship with Moscow. In Washington, U.S. officials, including President Jimmy Carter, expressed these concerns to Vice Premier Deng who, nonetheless, refrained from committing himself on China's intended course of action in Indochina. Enroute home, Deng stopped in Tokyo for talks with the Japanese – who likewise counseled restraint. Within days of Deng's return to China, Chinese troops crossed the PRC's southern border to "teach Vietnam a lesson."

The main lesson perceived by much of the rest of the world and the Third World in particular was that Beijing had been able to gain the approval of both Washington and Tokyo for the Chinese military action. Moscow, already alarmed by what it denounced as a developing Sino-U.S.-Japanese alliance, responded to the situation by increasing its military commitments to Vietnam. In the months that followed, international events, in particular the December 1979 Soviet invasion of Afghanistan and deliberations over the possibility of U.S. arms transfers to China, continued to strengthen the Sino-U.S. relationship. Deng put further strains on the Sino-Soviet angle of the triangle in early 1980 by adopting, albeit briefly, a public policy line that called for the broadest possible international united front against the Soviet Union— an informal alliance under U.S. military leadership.

China's efforts to position itself as leader of the Third World will have a significant impact on the PRC's relations with both the United States and the USSR in coming years. Like a politician out of office, China frequently finds it possible to oppose both U.S. and Soviet policies or actions in the Third World while avoiding specific counsel on how particular problems could be solved. If history is any indicator, moreover, China will find it extremely difficult to balance its position between the United States and the Soviet Union, although such a balance is obviously in China's interest. Fears incubated in centuries of invasion from the north, unsettled border disputes with the Soviet Union, disagreements between rival communist parties—including deep Chinese resentment over "betrayal" by Moscow in 1960—and greater availability of modernization assistance from the West all militate against an equidistance from both Washington and Moscow.

2

Relations with the Third World: 1949–1981

Basic Concepts of Chinese Foreign Policy

Since 1949, five ideological concepts, basically consistent but with changing applications, have guided China's relations with the Third World. These are (1) the theory of contradictions, (2) the concept of the united front, (3) the concept of the centrality of armed struggle to political victory, (4) the principle of self-reliance, and (5) the concept of China as a model for development. The variety of foreign policy tools and tactics taken up, laid down, and sometimes taken up again as China has sought to enhance its international position are all related to these basic concepts.

Three major doctrines – the doctrine of People's War, the Five Principles of Peaceful Coexistence, and the Three Worlds theory – have evolved from the five primary ideological concepts as principal guideposts in China's relationship with the Third World. The doctrine of People's War, presented in fully developed form in Defense Minister Lin Piao's 1965 article, "Long Live the Victory of People's War," had been a core concept in Maoist revolutionary thought since the early days of the CCP. The Five Principles of Peaceful Coexistence were officially adopted by the PRC at the first significant Third World gathering – the 1955 Bandung Conference of Asian and African states. The Three Worlds theory, although foreshadowed in earlier periods, was formally set forth by Beijing in a 1974 statement by Vice Premier Deng before the UN General Assembly and expanded upon in a key *People's Daily* editorial in November 1977.

Theory of Contradictions

Central to the application of Chinese foreign policy in whatever period has been the theory of contradictions. As outlined by Mao in 1937 in his essay "On Contradiction," this central dictum defines the crucial role of conflict in political affairs, going beyond the principle of pragmatism evident in any state's foreign relations. Central to the implementation of the theory is the ability to identify the main contradiction of any given time or situation. All other issues (contradictions) may then be subordinated to policies aimed at solving this main contradiction.

Using the theory of contradictions, Beijing has been able to pursue foreign policy tactics that appear mutually contradictory but are in fact intended to advance international conditions toward an ultimate goal of Chinese primacy in the Third World. Thus, for example, during the 1960s China emphasized active and open support of international revolution while still claiming general adherence to the principle of noninterference in other countries' internal affairs and maintaining diplomatic ties with the very governments whose overthrow was sought. The concept has enabled Beijing to maintain its doctrine that revolution is not exportable, while at various times making strenuous efforts to encourage revolution, and to insist on an internal policy of self-reliance while still providing foreign aid. Similarly, while adhering to rigid dogmas of what constitutes true socialism, in practice the PRC has through the years demonstrated considerable flexibility in its relationships with nonsocialist Third World states. In the early 1960s, "the Sino-Indian dispute prompted Beijing to denounce Indian socialism as fraudulent, but no attacks were made on such notions as 'African socialism' and 'Arab socialism.'"[7]

The United Front

The united front concept, employed by the Chinese Communists since the 1920s, basically posits the advisability of uniting with the lesser enemy against the greater as in the united front with the Kuomintang against the Japanese during World War II. Integral to the Three Worlds theory, the united front concept has been advanced by China on an international level since the late 1940s, although with various interpretations depending upon China's internal political current. Thus, for example, Beijing supported the Algerian nationalists in a non-Communist united front against the French in the Algerian war for independence and since the mid-1950s has advocated Arab unity against Israel. But China has denounced as bogus Cuban and Soviet efforts to unite nationalist groups in Latin America and Africa. For a brief period following the 1979 Soviet invasion of Afghanistan, Beijing even took the extraordinary step of publicly advocating an informal anti-Soviet front, with China and the Third World aligned on the side of the United States.[8]

Armed Struggle

The concept of the centrality of armed struggle to political victory grew out of China's experiences during the eight-year struggle against Japan and the civil war between the Nationalists and the Communists that followed. Armed struggle is, moreover, the most important of the five basic concepts as it arises out of the presence of contradiction, depends for its success on correct application of the united front and of self-reliance, and provides to the world what many modern Chinese regard as China's greatest contribution to mankind, the model road to national independence.

Publication in 1965 of Lin Piao's article, "Long Live the Victory of People's War," was the high point for the doctrine of the centrality of armed struggle. According to Lin, " . . . the contemporary world revolution . . . presents a picture of the encirclement of the cities by the rural areas. In the final analysis, the whole course of world revolution hinges on the revolutionary struggles of the Asian, African and Latin American peoples." More specifically, "As for revolutionary wars waged by the oppressed nations and peoples, so far from opposing them, we invariably give them firm support and active aid." Simply put, Lin called for universal revolution in which the "cities of the world," meaning the developed areas, would be encircled and overcome by the world's "rural areas,": the underdeveloped world.

In essence, the article contained nothing new, merely underlining in six points the guiding precepts of the Chinese revolution as formulated and carried out by Mao in previous years.[9] It was the timing of Lin's article that was all important, coming as the Cultural Revolution began and confirming China's position as a supporter of revolutionary armed struggle leading to an international Communist victory. Although the article was published essentially for an internal audience whose support Mao sought in his efforts to retain party control and although the publication of a statement on People's War did not result in profound changes in Chinese global activities, the article was regarded by governments throughout the world, by China's neighbors in particular, as a manual for international revolutionary action.

Much of its significance lay in the importance attached

to it by those who feared China's intentions but had insufficient grasp of China's potential or even of China's actual objectives. Appearing at a time of increased domestic radicalism and emerging Chinese policies of active confrontation on the diplomatic level, Lin's manifesto raised fears of a Chinese capability to foment revolution on a broad international scale. Although this fear never materialized, suspicions of application of the People's War theory continue to influence the PRC's ties with both the developed and developing worlds.

A key element in the Sino-Soviet ideological split in the late 1950s was Moscow's decision – in view of the dangers of a nuclear era unforeseen by Lenin – to begin stressing a pro-peace policy, which called for détente with the West and provided less support for world revolution. With the passing of time and changing of international circumstances, China has today arrived at a very similar position. In the 1970s the Three Worlds theory and the doctrine of the united front provided China the rationale, under changed world conditions, for backing off on its own support for revolution, People's War, and armed struggle. Then, as China began to consider the Soviet Union the greatest threat to international security, Beijing also began to seek détente with the West. Finally, in the most recent foreign policy shift, that of the early 1980s, China has begun, albeit with continued ambiguity, to stress the need for a pro-peace policy over the policy of "antihege-monism," that is, struggle, including armed struggle.[10]

Thus, although People's War or the revolutionary style of armed conflict remains of necessity a tenet of the PRC's defense strategy, whether such a policy is realistic is currently being debated. Beyond China, Beijing concentrates on diplomatic ties and downplays world revolution. But People's War is still regarded as a correct tactic in selected localities including Kampuchea, Afghanistan, and, in tandem with efforts to negotiate, southern Africa and Palestine.

Self-Reliance

The principle of self-reliance has not usually required complete rejection of outside economic assistance nor refusal of all international agreements or alliances. It is, however, a principle intended to remind of the dangers that lurk in the dependence that grows out of alliance with and acceptance of aid from stronger states. The principle has, moreover, the advantage of excusing China from major assistance programs to other developing countries unless there are political reasons for an exception to be made.

Adoption by China of the principle of self-reliance as central to its foreign policy pronouncements and practices reflects the history of China as well as the history of the CCP. During the past several decades self-reliance has served as a shibboleth in internal policy debates and is, in fact, a central stated guideline for the PRC's current modernization program despite the economic open door to the West.

Model for Development

Also fundamental to China's foreign policy has been the idea of China as a role model. First articulated by CCP second-in-command Liu Shaoqi in Moscow in 1949 when he described the Chinese revolution as a model for underdeveloped and colonialist-dominated Asian and African countries, the concept includes the notion of both revolutionary modernization and revolutionary armed struggle. Central to this idea of role model is the concept of China as elder brother, whose bitter experience has equipped it to show the way to other underdeveloped countries oppressed by imperialists and colonialists.

Beijing's promotion of China as a model has at times been more implicit than explicit, and the concept has been deemphasized since the end of the Cultural Revolution. The Chinese have usually been careful to point out to Third World countries that the Chinese revolutionary model does not on all points correspond to conditions and experiences of other states. There has probably always been considerably more Third World interest in China's role as an agricultural country seeking modernization than in other aspects of the Chinese model. Nonetheless, Beijing has at times overreached itself in attempting to apply the armed struggle aspect of the model. During the Cultural Revolution, tribesmen in Oman's Dhofar province were portrayed in Beijing's foreign language media as patterning their lives around devotion to Chairman Mao. And, according to Mohammed Heikal, Egyptian President Gamal Abd-al-Nasser's biographer, Mao exhorted Egypt in 1967 to carry on a people's war in the Sinai following the Egyptian defeat by the Israelis and had to be reminded by Nasser that there are "no people" in the Sinai.

Policy: Evolution and Continuity

Over the years the five basic concepts and the three fundamental doctrines that have grown from them have been emphasized or ignored in accordance with Beijing's interpretation of international events. As indicated, the concepts of armed struggle and the Chinese model for development have diminished in importance since the end of the Cultural Revolution and self-reliance has been subject to reinterpretation. These reinterpretations have caused the doctrine of People's War to lose its ideological and global importance so that today it is applied selectively by China only on a case-by-case basis.

Although Beijing claims continued adherence to the Three Worlds theory—which is useful from the standpoint of the stress it places on China's willingness to work with all governments—the theory is a malleable doctrine and evolution continues in its application. The Five Principles of

Peaceful Coexistence appears once again to be enjoying a rise in popularity under the new independent policy. Although Beijing would deny any conflict between the Three Worlds theory and the Five Principles of Peaceful Coexistence, clearly the latter is considerably less confrontationist than the former.

The implications for China's Third World relationships are significant. A decline in the importance of the concept of armed struggle and the doctrine of People's War means more stable state-to-state relations as China's support for revolution decreases. Less emphasis on the Three Worlds theory would allow Beijing greater flexibility in selection and support of international issues as the united front concept is de-emphasized in favor of policy independence. Such selectivity may, indeed, be the direction in which China is moving – a position well supported by the vague but positive Five Principles of Peaceful Coexistence.

Since the late 1970s, public Chinese statements have not stressed the centrality of the Three Worlds theory for Chinese foreign policy, despite continuing emphasis on the importance of the Third World to China's international position. This disparity appears to reflect a debate within the Chinese leadership over how completely China should pin its policy to the effort to influence the Third World. Included in the debate are the questions of how realistically Beijing's Third World ambitions are as well as how the Second and Third Worlds relate to one another. (Beijing's efforts to encourage Western European "independence" from the United States is indicative of a desire to muster all nations against superpower domination.)

Nonetheless, although Beijing seldom mentions the Three Worlds theory, neither has it repudiated the concept. The July 1981 sixth plenum of the eleventh party congress included the Three Worlds theory in its list of Mao's achievements.

Speaking to the UN General Assembly in September 1977, Chinese Foreign Minister Huang Hua said that "The great significance of this thesis lies in the fact that it provides the people of the world with a powerful ideological instrument with which to identify the main revolutionary forces, the chief enemies, and the middle forces that can be won over within the international struggle today."[11] Many Chinese leaders continue to regard the Three Worlds theory as a powerful lever to Third World influence because it provides for China the opportunity "to participate in defining the terms of global order."[12]

China's Foreign Policy Before the Cultural Revolution

The PRC's pre-Cultural Revolution foreign policy can be divided into three periods: 1949–1953, 1954–1959, and 1960–1965. Although each period had a different specific emphasis, the major catalysts for Chinese tactics and policy were inevitably a combination of internal domestic considerations and China's relationships with Moscow and Washington.

During each of these periods, however, Beijing found its Third World ties of immense relevance to the fundamental issues of security and recognition, which motivate Chinese foreign policy and infuse the PRC's relations with the developed world. Developments within the Third World itself, in particular the appearance of newly independent nations, contributed to Beijing's perception of opportunity and hence to policy formulation. The specific actions of Third World states – internal corruption and power struggles, requests for development funds, efforts to use China as a counter to Soviet or U.S. manipulation – served to stimulate China's policy.

1949–1953: "Leaning to One Side" or the Politics of Communist Internationalism

The years immediately following 1949 found Beijing preoccupied with internal problems, chiefly those of national unification, and somewhat uncertain over how to proceed on the international level. A close relationship was maintained with the Soviet Union as leader of world communism, although seeds of discord were steadily growing. Relations with the United States were never worse than during this early era, which included armed confrontation during the 1950–1953 Korean War.

China's need to concentrate on internal developments was complemented by the desire to consolidate ties with the Communist world and to encourage the spread of communism to neighboring countries. Under the leadership of Mao Zedong, Liu Shaoqi, Deng Xiaoping, and Zhou Enlai, the PRC sought to enhance its international security with diplomatic ties with Communist states in tandem with a policy of advocating revolutionary armed struggle in non-Communist countries.

Decolonization was still the major preoccupation of Third World countries, and China offered itself as a model for liberation. In agreement with the Soviet "two camp" theory, first put forward at a Cominform meeting in September 1947, China "leaned" toward the side of international communism to combat the forces of colonialism and imperialism. Unlike the blind eye that Beijing has in later years often turned to the excesses and failures of Third World states, in the early 1950s China was openly critical of other Third World countries' foreign and domestic policies that were not in accordance with its own. Such criticism undoubtedly arose from feelings of satisfaction over the CCP's victory at home, but they also reflected Beijing's international isolation resulting in large part from U.S. opposition to international acceptance of the Chinese Communist regime.

Because of internal preoccupation during this period and lack of wide-ranging international ties, China's efforts to instigate revolution were primarily geared toward the Asian states. In the late 1940s and early 1950s, Chinese influence contributed to insurrections in several Asian states including Burma, India, Malaya, the Philippines, and Indonesia. Material aid to external revolutionary movements was of necessity extremely limited during this period, even though, as recipients of Soviet aid, the Chinese did not unduly emphasize the policy of self-reliance, which later became so prominent in Beijing's pronouncements.

Although in the early 1950s China based its domestic policy on a united front strategy with the "national bourgeoisie," Mao feared such a policy on an international scale, believing political neutrality to be impossible and seeing the world largely in terms of black and white. Internationally, therefore, Mao sought to concentrate on developing ties with Communist states and with Communist groups, rejecting Indian Prime Minister Jawaharlal Nehru's suggestion that India and China act together to form a "third force" between the two superpowers.

By 1951, although the Chinese leadership was still deeply suspicious of other non-Communist countries, changes had begun to occur. These were evident in China's verbal support for Iranian plans to nationalize foreign oil concessions and for Egypt's anti-British policies. The 1952 convening by China of a "Peace Conference of the Asian and Pacific Region," which included several Latin American states, also reflected progress toward a policy that would allow China to seek greater international support from and alignment with non-Communist states of the developing world. Indicative of this policy rethinking was the absence of theoretical pronouncements on neutrality or Third World leadership in the Chinese media between late 1952 and early 1954.[13]

Credit for the perception that China could benefit from

anti-imperialist and anticolonialist positions adopted by neutral or non-Communist forces appears to belong to Zhou Enlai, who, during nearly a quarter of a century as premier or foreign minister (or sometimes both), sought the establishment of a broad united front against imperialism. Zhou's objectives were both the enhancement of China's international influence and the establishment of a "neutral belt of states as the 'zone of peace' between the western coalition and China."[14] The phrase "peaceful coexistence," although of Leninist origin, was first used by Zhou in February 1953 in his political report to the national Committee of the People's Political Consultative Conference.

In the early 1950s Zhou was able to redefine "neutrality," at least temporarily, as opposition to U.S. influence and rejection of anti-Chinese alliances – rather than as anti-Communist. It is possible he was influenced by Nasser's concept of "positive neutralism," which likewise advocated Third World distancing from East-West politics. The move toward acceptance of peaceful coexistence and even possible cooperation with non-Communist states signaled an evolution in Beijing's foreign policy and brought a consequent deemphasis on the centrality of armed struggle – leading into the Bandung era.

1954–1959: "Peaceful Coexistence"
in the Bandung Era

The second period of Chinese foreign policy, in which China officially took "peaceful coexistence" as its watchword, saw increased Chinese diplomatic efforts to influence Third World governments. China's opportunity was provided by the April 1955 Conference of Asian Countries in New Delhi, followed that same month by the Conference of Asian and African states at Bandung, Indonesia. Formation of the Afro-Asian People's Solidarity Organization (AAPSO) in Cairo in 1958 also provided expanded possibilities for Chinese efforts to gain international influence.

From November 1956 through January 1957, Zhou Enlai visited eight Asian states, extolling the Five Principles of Peaceful Coexistence, which had been adopted at Bandung as responsible international behavior.[15] Meanwhile, the PRC began to expand its ties elsewhere as well, establishing diplomatic relations with a variety of Middle Eastern and African countries. The Third World, the Asian states in particular, greeted with relief a "new China," which announced its desire to seek political solutions to common problems rather than work toward destabilization or revolution.

Domestic events continued to shape foreign policy during the late 1950s as the anti-rightist campaign enhanced the position of the more militant elements inside the Chinese hierarchy and tensions increased between Beijing and Moscow. Increased feelings of isolation contributed to political belligerence in Beijing. Despite the slogan of "peaceful coexistence," the PRC gradually began to reemphasize the armed struggle aspect of its foreign policy. The late 1950s saw a hardening of the Chinese anti-UN position, as illustrated in rhetoric over the 1958 Middle East crisis, as well as a deterioration of relations with Asian states following the 1958 Sino-Indian border clashes.

The late 1950s thus mark a turning point in China's foreign relations, following which China moved rapidly away from the Bandung spirit although not the letter and became considerably more militant. By 1958 the Chinese leadership had returned to its earlier skepticism on the value of neutrality, once again defining the East-West conflict as basically a class struggle. The Chinese conclusion in the late 1950s that true peaceful coexistence was not only impossible but that active Chinese support for revolutionary struggle was essential was distasteful to Third World states, as was the PRC's identification of its own experience with other countries' national struggles. According to China specialist Charles Neuhauser,

> The Chinese have often overlooked the specifics of a given situation for more generalized revolutionary pronouncements. They have confused local rebellion with genuine national revolutionary movement. Indeed, one looks in vain for discussion of Africa and the Middle East in terms of Marxian class analysis. . . . Moreover, Peking apparently has a tendency to see analogies to the Chinese experience where they do not in fact exist.[16]

A series of events may be cited for loss of Chinese credibility in the Third World after 1957, most of them chargeable to Chinese political rigidity and diplomatic heavy handedness. Contributing to Beijing's loss of advantage in the Third World were (1) opposition to China's revolutionary line by nationalist governments already in power, (2) Chinese attacks on Yugoslavia for its "neutralism," (3) a late 1959 dispute with Indonesia over Chinese residents there, (4) deterioration of Sino-Indian relations over Tibet and actual combat with India over border questions in 1958 (and more seriously in 1962), and (5) controversy with Egypt over the suppression of Communists in Egypt and Nasser's support for anti-Communist activities in Iraq. By 1960 China found itself virtually isolated from all important non-Communist Third World countries, including those that it had impressed at Bandung in 1955 by statements on China's commitment to peaceful coexistence.

1960–1965: "The East Wind Prevails over the West Wind"—Antirevisionism and Anti-imperialism

The 1960s was a decade of confrontation. Following the open break between China and the Soviet Union, the PRC increased its efforts to achieve influence in the Third World at both Soviet and U.S. expense, adopting an "independent" foreign policy strategy that described Asia, Africa, and Latin America as "the focus of world contradictions" and the "storm center of the world revolution."

The Sino-Soviet split left China feeling even more isolated in what it perceived as a very hostile world. During the early 1960s, moreover, "Mao's preoccupation with the future of the Chinese revolution typified an indecisive search for new direction within the Party as a whole."[17] Mao responded in 1964 with a restatement of his 1946 division of the world into two "intermediate zones."[18] A precursor to the Three Worlds theory, this simple division of the world into developing zone and developed zone called for unity of the two zones to form a "third force," which would oppose superpower efforts to achieve international control.

As it entered into rivalry with the Soviet Union for control of Communist movements and international organizations worldwide, China stridently opposed the Soviet position that the Cold War and the arms race should be ended in order to benefit Third World economic development. Rather, Beijing believed, the underdeveloped world should rally behind China's revolutionary leadership in its promotion of national liberation struggles. A frequent Chinese theme was that Moscow had abdicated its responsibility to use its military capability to serve as guarantor of anti-imperialist struggles. At this time, Beijing also began actively to oppose superpower and Second World economic supremacy and to call for radical changes, a concept that remains a central component of Chinese foreign policy pronouncements under the guise of a new international economic order.

The choice of opposition to colonialism and imperialism as specific issues around which to mobilize Third World support had been favorably received by the Third World in the 1950s. But by the 1960s, the Chinese philosophy of Third World self-reliance and Chinese antisuperpower rhetoric had become unappealing to the newly emerging states of Africa and Asia. The notion of China as a revolutionary model, another attempted rallying point of support used by Beijing, was likewise distasteful as the new and developing nations were far less interested in international power struggles than in getting on with domestic development, often with aid acquired from those described by China as enemies and exploiters. Chinese inflexibility on the issue of "neutrality" — a country was either for or against China — further restricted the PRC's influence.

Yet, desiring to counter Soviet advances, China redoubled its efforts to find allies in the Third World. The Chinese Asia-Africa Society was formed in May 1959 to aid in the push to strengthen ties with Third World governments. In 1964 and 1965, Zhou made two extensive tours of Africa during which he promoted Beijing's stated ideals of anti-imperialism, antirevisionism, and Asian-African unity. There was little that China could hope to gain economically from ties with weak and often impoverished Third World states. But Beijing's major goal was simply to counter the growth of U.S. and Soviet influence. The PRC's approach during this period has been described as "the development of 'bargain basement' methods of influencing Asian, African, and even Latin American countries by economic and technical assistance and by advice on guerrilla warfare and political and economic policy."[19]

At the same time China maintained and sought to expand relations with a variety of African revolutionary organizations, a policy that was in the late 1950s and early 1960s "fragmentary and opportunistic in the extreme," leading China to extend support to groups that were nonviable and those that had little chance for success.[20] This opportunistic and revolutionary policy placed considerable strain on China's diplomatic relations in the region. In the long run, China's promotion of revolution in Africa was successful only in regard to Algeria, to whose nationalist leadership China had provided support since the late 1950s and which gained its independence in 1962.

The Afro-Asian People's Solidarity Organization became a special arena for Sino-Soviet rivalry, resulting in bitter public quarrels between the Chinese and the Soviets and their respective supporters. Chinese efforts centered on condemnation of the Soviet formulas for coexistence and disarmament, promotion of Chinese positions on armed struggle and national liberation, and condemnation of the Soviets as both racist and non-Asian and therefore not by rights members of the AAPSO.

The second AAPSO conference, which was to have been held in Algiers in 1964, was permanently postponed – to the relief of several countries – by the Algerian coup that replaced Ahmed Ben Bella with Houari Boumedienne. The haste with which China recognized the new regime in an effort to reschedule the AAPSO conference, despite long ties with Ben Bella, was distasteful to several African governments and provided further impetus for a decline in Chinese influence in Africa.

The Chinese tended to concentrate their efforts in Africa on those few governments that appeared to Beijing to have the greatest possibility for socialist revolution. These governments included those of Mali, Ghana, Guinea, and Algeria, the leaders of all of which soon passed from political power taking with them any immediate hopes for increased Chinese influence. Moreover, the oppositionist groups supported by China during this period uniformly failed to come to power. In the mid-1960s Chinese diplomats were expelled from Burundi on charges of using the country as a base to sponsor rebellion in Congo/Kinshasa (now Zaire), as well as from Niger, Dahomey (Benin), the Central African Republic, and Ghana on charges of engaging in subversive activities.

In addition to Africa, Beijing also sought to broaden its contacts in Latin America where, as elsewhere, China's major goal was to counter Soviet influence. With the exception of Cuba, however, diplomatic ties were not established between China and any Latin American country in the early 1960s. Because Cuba was a proto-Communist state, the choice of Cuba was possibly more understandable, but the seeds of the Sino-Cuban rift were soon apparent. Although China saw Castro's successful rise to power as a foothold for communism in the Western hemisphere, Beijing resented his growing reliance on Moscow and his efforts to present the Cuban, rather than the Chinese, revolutionary model to Latin America. Seeking to exploit Soviet-Cuban difficulties during the 1962 Cuban missile crisis between the United States and the USSR, Beijing verbally supported Cuba, accusing Moscow of a "Munich policy."

During the 1960s "there was not an armed movement of any consequence in Latin America that did not receive at least implicit support from Peking."[21] Yet most of these contacts were inconsequential, despite major Chinese attention to visits by representatives of a variety of splinter groups and Maoist parties; rhetoric in support of agrarian unrest in such countries as Bolivia, Columbia, and Peru; and praise for Panama in its disputes with the United States.

To facilitate acceptance of Chinese Third World leadership ambitions, during the early 1960s Beijing established such groups as the Sino-Latin American Friendship Association and the Chinese-African Friendship Association, a subsidiary of the Chinese Peoples Association for Friendship with Foreign Countries. But China completely failed to establish a position of authority inside any influential Third World group or organization or to organize a 1965 Afro-Asian summit conference.[22] By 1967 the Chinese and their few supporters had lost administrative influence even in the AAPSO. When the first African-Asian-Latin American People's Solidarity conference was held in Havana in January 1966, Soviet maneuvers prevented China from obtaining any degree of influence in that organization.

By 1965 a series of miscalculations and adventures in both Africa and Asia had brought further serious setbacks to China's ties with the Third World. In Asia these setbacks included increased regional suspicion of China as a result of the 1962 border conflict with India and the 1965 break in diplomatic relations with Indonesia following a Communist-inspired coup attempt. China, moreover, had no diplomatic ties and little contact with several major Asian states including Japan, Thailand, the Philippines, Malaysia, and South Korea. The only real Asian success for China during this period was the beginning of the long and mutually beneficial friendship with Pakistan, whereby China sought to counter closer Soviet-Indian ties and Pakistan sought to hedge itself against the Indian threat.[23]

China's tilt toward a more militant policy coincided with the growth of independent governments in Asia and Africa, governments that for reasons of their own objected to the Chinese rhetoric on self-reliance, now emphasized because of China's loosened ties to Moscow, which would deny them the foreign aid and UN membership they sought. Furthermore, the "united front from below" policy that allowed China simultaneously to contact and support groups that sought the overthrow of legitimate governments with which China had diplomatic ties proved anathema to several African states.

Thus, the radical nature of Chinese policy and Beijing's failure to understand the dynamics of African culture, nationalism, history, and politics combined to cause China's initiatives to self-destruct in Africa in the late 1950s and early 1960s. The Africans, as well as other Third World groups, were annoyed by the spectacle of the Sino-Soviet dispute and vigorously resisted attempts to get them involved. According to China scholar George Yu, writing in 1966, China's failure in Africa was primarily due to

... the basic incompatibility between Chinese foreign policy objectives and the goals of the African states.

Verbally, China has supported Africa's quest for political and economic independence and international acceptance and recognition, but actually she has attempted to
induce the African states to accept fully her world view
and major policy objectives. This the vast majority of
the African states have been unwilling to do.[24]

At home, moreover, discord in the leadership following
the failure of the Great Leap Forward (1957) and the Hundred Flowers Campaign (1958) and political differences resulting from the first five-year economic plan (1953–1957) were
about to lead into the chaos of the Cultural Revolution. By
1966, the Cultural Revolution's turmoil had brought the recall
of all Chinese ambassadors with the exception of Huang Hua
in Cairo. And by 1968 China's foreign policy had come to a
virtual standstill, the economy was in chaos, and it seemed
that the Chinese Communist experiment was in the process
of destroying itself.

People's War and the Cultural Revolution

Cultural Revolution foreign policy was chiefly a reflection
of events inside China, with no overall planning. Beijing's major focus during the period was on internal problems – the power struggle that threatened to undo the Chinese revolution –
and not on external relations. The famed doctrine of People's
War, articulated by Lin Piao in 1965, mirrored the preoccupation with ideology that during this period saw the evilness
of Soviet "revisionism" surpass that of U.S. imperialism.

Yet although the Cultural Revolution had more to do
with domestic than with foreign concerns, the two were in-
tricately connected. As Mao sought to retain his authority
in the face of opposition from such formidable party figures
as Liu Shaoqi, tellingly dubbed "China's Khrushchev," the

world was treated to the spectacle of internal Chinese politics, previously debated behind closed doors, played out on the international stage. Mass rallies and attacks on foreign diplomatic missions in Beijing led to agitation and violence by Chinese diplomats abroad, the listing by the PRC of countries (many of them in the Third World) as "targets of revolution," and the closing of Chinese diplomatic missions in several countries.

Between the late 1950s and 1969, diplomatic relations were ruptured or suspended with six countries, all in the Third World (Burundi, the Central African Republic, Dahomey, Ghana, Indonesia, and Tunisia). Interestingly, China did not itself formally initiate a break in relations with any country during the Cultural Revolution or, on the basis of principle, stop trading with any "revisionist" or "imperialist" countries, a point that reinforces the domestic nature of the Chinese outburst.

It is significant, moreover, that throughout the Cultural Revolution Chinese material support for revolutionary groups did not increase, although verbal support for such groups shot up dramatically. The constraints of poverty, distance, and internal preoccupation served to prevent greater international revolutionary involvement. It does appear, however, that behind the increasing revolutionary rhetoric in the early 1960s Beijing did make an effort to learn from some of its Third World failures.

By 1965 Beijing had become somewhat more selective in determining what national revolutionary groups and causes to support explicitly. Following the failure of various African groups that had received Chinese sponsorship, particularly those interested in quick coups, and the consequent damage to China's position in Africa, there was a Chinese tendency by the mid-1960s toward support of those groups that showed evidence of mass appeal, whose strategy was long term rather than based on coups, whose programs had a chance for success, and whose objectives lay in an area in which China's state-to-state ties would not be harmed.

Peter Van Ness differentiates between implicit and explicit Chinese support during this period, explicit recognition (sometimes including diplomatic status) going to pro-Beijing Communist parties and selected groups such as the South Vietnamese National Liberation Front and the Palestine Liberation Organization (PLO) and broad implicit support mainly in the form of media pronouncements to practically all other groups leading armed revolutions or claiming to represent oppressed people – including American blacks and the peoples of Japan, the Congo, the Dominican Republic, and Panama. Interestingly, in view of the coming rift between China and the world, fear of damaging China's diplomatic ties still kept Beijing from endorsing wars of "national liberation" in several areas, including French Somaliland, Kenya, Kashmir, Burma, and Indonesia in 1965.[25]

Several characteristics of China's Cultural Revolution policy merit closer examination. As a consequence of the emphasis on ideological purity, China increased its support for a variety of Maoist groups and organizations seeking revolution in various parts of the world. The Chinese also engaged in vicious verbal attacks on Third World countries such as Burma, which only shortly before it had lauded as close friends. There was, further, an increased emphasis on the revolutionary role to be played – in Beijing's view – by overseas Chinese communities that, sometimes actively during the period, played out the Maoist philosophy.

These three issues – support for splinter and antigovernment groups, irresponsible diplomatic behavior, and claims to a special relationship with overseas Chinese – continue to have a significant impact on the attitudes of some Third World, particularly Asian, countries toward China. Fears raised by China's behavior during the Cultural Revolution revived historical suspicions of China and will take many years to eradicate. China today is sensitive to this legacy and

at times goes out of its way to seek to assuage fears that it
will some day revert to similar patterns. The *Beijing Review*
in an early 1984 commentary on China's diplomacy asserted
that "the policy of opening to the rest of the world is a component of China's foreign diplomacy. . . . the door which has
been opened will never close. . . . China acts according to
established international practices."

Finally, promotion of the doctrine of People's War during the Cultural Revolution caused serious damage to China's
Third World standing. Lin Piao's article, "Long Live the Victory of People's War," compared the "world countryside" of
Asia, Africa, and Latin America to the "world cities" of North
America and Western Europe, which the Third World was
urged to surround and capture. The PRC had long supported
armed struggle to achieve revolutionary gains. Why then did
China decide in the mid-1960s to wage ideological war on the
world? How and why did it happen that by late 1967 China
had become involved in controversies, often quite serious,
with more than 30 countries?

The answer lies in a combination of internal political
disagreements and disappointments over world events that
had left China feeling increasingly isolated and vulnerable.
Internally, the watchword was "self-reliance." Internationally,
the main response was the doctrine of People's War, which,
Beijing believed, responded to several of the PRC's basic concerns. In lashing out against isolation and sounding cries of
alarm about the international dangers posed by Soviet revisionism and U.S. imperialism, China reflected its concerns
for its own security. The formulation of a "new" theory based
on China's revolutionary experience gave further impetus to
China's perception of its rightful role as an international
model for revolution. And the act of precipitating action and
crisis provided China's leaders with feelings of significance
and of recognition crucial to their sense of China's worth as
a nation.

Nonetheless, Mao's basic motivation in the Cultural Revolution was internal control rather than external revolution. Success in the latter would be regarded by Mao mainly as confirmation of his right to domestic authority. On the eve of the Cultural Revolution, as Mao was preparing his daring attempt to neutralize party opposition to his economic and social policies, the U.S.bombing of North Vietnam and the subsequent acceleration of the U.S. involvement with China's neighbor caused a major debate among China's leaders over how best to respond to this new threat to China's security.

Publication of Lin's article calling for a Third World revolutionary struggle against the superpowers – with a concurrent message about the importance of self-reliance – was probably intended as a warning to Vietnam that China would continue its material and verbal support for Vietnam but would not, as it had done in Korea, commit Chinese troops against the United States on foreign soil. The message was phrased in such a way as to put the world on notice that China was capable of lashing out against what it considered encroachments on its security and interests, warning the United States in particular that China was a force to be reckoned with in Asia. But the adopting of a belligerent posture served the domestic purpose of rallying support behind the Maoist faction, while the principle of self-reliance justified Chinese nonintervention outside the PRC, thus allowing a concentration of energy on the Cultural Revolution.

According to Asian scholar Chalmers Johnson, Mao's desire to elevate the anticolonialist struggle to "historical significance" in its own right lies at the ideological base of People's War.[26] In other words, by pushing this ideological development, Mao hoped to exploit discontent in the Third World, to promote his cause as a revolutionary innovator both at home and abroad, and to confront the Soviet position that peaceful transition to socialism was possible.

The years 1969–1971 were a transition from China's revolutionary to postrevolutionary foreign policies. As the Cultural Revolution ended, China once again shifted greater weight to diplomatic ties and in so doing reduced both aid and verbal support for revolutionary movements and groups. Beijing's primary preoccupation during this time was to end its international isolation in a world in which the strategic power balance appeared to be shifting dangerously in favor of the Soviet Union. The ninth party congress held in April 1969 signaled an end to the most violent stage of the Cultural Revolution, and by May 1969 the PRC had begun to reestablish diplomatic relations with the rest of the world.[27] By 1971 China had gained the support needed for admission to the UN.

The August 1968 Soviet invasion of Czechoslovakia is generally credited with turning China away from international belligerence and isolation. The specter of the Soviet invasion of a fellow Communist state through application of the Brezhnev Doctrine clearly contributed to a new Chinese openness to the West, which soon became evident. But the achievement of his domestic aims also influenced Mao's policy decision as once again he felt himself in a position of enhanced authority due to the successful discrediting of his major opponents within the Chinese Communist Party.

Meanwhile, President Lyndon Johnson's peace offer to Vietnam was seen by Beijing as the welcome release of U.S. pressure at a time when Sino-Soviet relations were worsening dramatically. In late November 1968 the PRC proposed resumption of the sporadic Warsaw talks with the United States, and, although the talks did not in fact resume until January 1970, the train of events leading to the 1972 Shanghai Communiqué and the 1979 normalization of Sino-U.S. relations had begun.

Despite the fact that China's perception of a threat from the Soviet Union had been growing through the 1960s, China still described the United States as "the number one enemy" as late as the mid-1960s. One more indication of the impact of

Third World events on China's superpower relations was that, following the 1967 war in the Middle East, Beijing professed to see a convergence of U.S. and Soviet interests (against China as well as the rest of the Third World) and began to describe the two superpowers as "colluding" as well as "contending" for world domination. In September 1968, following the Soviet invasion of Czechoslovakia, Premier Zhou made the first Chinese reference to "Soviet social-imperialism," and Moscow became in China's view the greatest threat to world security. Not until late 1975, however, did the PRC begin to refer openly to the USSR as "the most dangerous source of world war."

Nonetheless, under Zhou's careful management, tensions between the Chinese and the Soviets were not allowed to get out of hand, although they came close to doing so. In a move to relieve serious tensions following Sino-Soviet border clashes in March 1969, the Chinese invited Soviet leader Alexsei Kosygin to visit Beijing in September. Bilateral talks between Moscow and Beijing began in October. This Chinese initiative also served to demonstrate to the Third World that the PRC was not interested in throwing itself into the U.S. "camp."

Willingness to talk was consistent with later maneuvers by Beijing to assume a more balanced position between the two superpowers. Such positioning can be seen as a compromise between those Chinese leaders who favored hostile equidistance and those who favored tilting toward the United States. Nonetheless, the next 10 years would see a basic trend of greater relative distancing from Moscow and the evolution of ties with the United States to the degree that, in April 1980, Deng Xiaoping would call publicly for a "long term, strategic relationship" with the United States, a move apparently aimed at achieving a de facto Sino-U.S. alliance. Deng, however, faced many opponents to such policy, in the Third World as well as in Beijing and Washington.

Post-Cultural Revolution Foreign Policy

The Soviet invasion of Czechoslovakia in 1968 and the wind-ing down of the Cultural Revolution after 1969 marked the beginning of a new era in China's foreign and domestic pol-icies. The major domestic issues under debate during the 1970s were the leadership succession to Mao, the problems of modernization and domestic recovery from the ravages of the Cultural Revolution, and, later in the decade, the correct interpretation of history, including Mao's role in the Cultural Revolution. Closely tied to these issues was the question of China's international position and what arrangements should be made to provide a secure environment in which to accom-plish domestic goals and gain foreign policy independence. Although factions in China's leadership differed widely over how such objectives were to be accomplished, there was a consensus that the PRC needed rapid resolution of the criti-cal domestic power struggle and security within a peaceful international environment.

The perception of a changed international geopolitical power balance in which the USSR was seen as ascendent over the United States made security Beijing's overriding concern. Moscow's application of the "Brezhnev doctrine" combined with growing Soviet pressure on China's borders reduced the threat of U.S. imperialism to a secondary position in relation to the dangers of Soviet hegemonism. Differences over how to manage the Soviet threat provided a backdrop for the looming problem of who would succeed the aging Mao.

Defense Minister Lin Piao made the first overt move. Although already officially designated Mao's successor, Lin feared Zhou's influence with Mao and opposed the late 1968 gestures toward the United States to counter the Soviet threat. Lin preferred continued opposition to both superpow-ers and hoped to maintain an internal atmosphere of urgency as a means of enhancing his own leadership position. Ties with the United States risked lessening this urgency, particularly if Washington began to be seen by other leadership elements as a shield for China.

Zhou, however, sought to take steps to return China to a more neutralist position such as he had pushed in the late 1950s Bandung era. As the struggle between the two approaches to security intensified, Mao went public in April 1971 with his efforts to establish ties with the United States by inviting the U.S. table tennis team to visit China. In so doing, Mao may have intended to derail Lin from an early power grab. The move served instead to intensify Lin's efforts, leading to what was apparently an abortive coup attempt in September and the death of Lin and a group of his chief supporters in a plane crash as they were reportedly fleeing to the Soviet Union.

Despite Lin's death, strong elements within the Chinese leadership continued to oppose "concessions" to the Soviets or to the United States, advocating instead a return to the belligerence and isolationism of the Cultural Revolution. The "Gang of Four," purged only after Mao's death in late 1976, was at the center of such efforts, resisting as well Zhou's opposition to their radical domestic programs and ambitions. A 1972 statement by Foreign Minister Qiao Guanhua at the UN General Assembly that China continued to adhere to the theory of "just wars" reflects this domestic debate over the direction of foreign policy and the value of confrontationism.

For nearly 40 years Zhou Enlai had served as the great mediator between factions in the Chinese Communist Party, and he will probably be remembered as the greatest Chinese statesman of the past two centuries. President Richard M. Nixon's February 1972 visit to Peking was perhaps the climax of Zhou's diplomatic efforts to move China away from isolationism. (From 1969–1971 it was between Zhou and the United States that Pakistan's President Yahya Khan carried secret messages. And it was Zhou again rather than Mao who figured principally in the 1971–1972 Beijing discussions with President Nixon and U.S. National Security Adviser Henry A. Kissinger.) But Zhou's objective was not alignment with Washington anymore than with Moscow. Following the border clashes in 1969, it was Zhou who pushed for the opening of talks with Moscow.

For Zhou Enlai, China's safest and wisest position was equidistance between the superpowers while strengthening ties with the Third World – permitting an independent, flexible foreign policy. The Bandung era, coming as it did before the Sino-Soviet split, was only a precursor to an era of greater international independence for the PRC. Allied to Moscow, Beijing could not adopt a truly neutral position. But neutrality was clearly Zhou's objective, and he moved with his remaining vigor in the early 1970s to accomplish this goal.

Deng Xioaping, whose drive for power brought him to a position of preeminence at the end of the 1970s, agreed with Zhou on the need to expand Third World ties. But Deng's main objective appears to have been the construction of a close relationship with the United States with which to counter the USSR. The early 1970s, however, was a time of compromise between Zhou and those leaders who advocated militancy in foreign policy as well as those who sought to tilt toward either superpower. Thus, as the internal power factions shifted before Mao's death in late 1976, radicalism and isolationism sometimes typified Beijing's statements and actions despite the influence of either Zhou or Deng. Not until the deaths of Mao and Zhou and the purge of the Gang of Four did Deng prevail – and then only imperfectly.

During the 1970s – as Deng struggled to gain influence, was purged a second time in the post-Mao power struggle, and then was once again rehabilitated – there was much talk of China as a Third World state and of construction of strong ties with the Third World to counter the superpowers. It was, in fact, Deng himself who first clearly articulated the Three

Worlds theory at the UN in 1974, declaring that "China will always remain a member of the Third World" and in effect setting the stage for the push for Third World leadership, which has only become fully visible some 10 years later.

But Deng's professed affinity for Chinese ties to the Third World may be interpreted in the context of his own domestic coalition building with Zhou's followers. Debate over the Chinese relationship with the Third World versus the strengthening of ties with the West played a major role in the internal policy debate during the entire decade. Deng's subsequent violations of the letter of the Three Worlds theory in his late 1970s' call for alliance with the United States to advance China's security and modernization revealed his intentions.

Before China could set a clear course for future international relations, the question of Mao's succession had to be settled. According to U.S. State Department China analyst Carol Lee Hamrin, two antagonistic power coalitions, the radical Maoists and the moderate Maoists, were identifiable in the mid-1970s.[28] Between these groups there was little cooperation or compromise as each sought to position itself to take over after Mao's demise. Zhou Enlai and Deng may be identified with the moderates and Hua Guofeng and Mao himself with the more radical group.

In April 1976, Deng—who held positions as CCP vice chairman, vice premier, and People's Liberation Army chief of staff, but had been deprived of protection by Zhou's death—was deposed for a second time by the radical group. Hua was given unexpected stature as premier and appointed to the Politburo Standing Committee. Although the threat of Deng was at least temporarily removed, Mao's coalition began to crumble as Mao's wife, Jiang Qing, and the other members of the Gang of Four sought to preempt Hua as heir-designate. This disunity and a series of shifting alliances accelerated with Mao's death in September 1976, leading to arrest of the

Gang of Four in October and Deng's rehabilitation in July 1977.

In the years since Deng's return, three power coalitions have emerged. There are, in Hamrin's terminology, the conservatives (Hua, Ye Jianying, and Li Xiannian), who have basically sought continuation of the less radical core of the mid-1970s Maoism; the pragmatic reformers (Deng, Hu Yaobang, and Zhao Ziyang), whose policies pointed toward greater reliance on the West and the movement of China toward a market-socialist economy; and a more orthodox reform group (Chen Yun and Peng Zhen), which sought a return to the foreign and domestic policies constructed by Zhou and Liu Shaoqi in the Bandung era.

As Deng gradually moved into ascendency over Hua at the third plenum of the eleventh party congress in December 1978 (Hua lost the prime ministership in 1980 and the CCP chairmanship in 1981), the orthodox group likewise moved to extend its authority. Through coalition building with the remnants of the conservative group, the orthodox group was able to deprive Deng of "an open mandate to depart further from China's Marxist-Leninist heritage."[29] The high tide of Deng's authority may thus be identified as 1978–1980, the years of greatest outreach toward the United States, including normalization of diplomatic relations in January 1979, and a concurrent downplaying of the importance of the Third World in China's international politics.

It was a foreign policy issue that provided the orthodox group the leverage it needed to derail Deng. That issue was the February 1979 Chinese invasion of Vietnam under Deng Xiaoping's authority as chief of staff. Following the invasion, Deng was strongly criticized for his policy orientation by those who preferred a more neutralist, less confrontational stance. Public statements by other Chinese leaders during this period reflected internal disagreement by stressing the need to align with "progressive forces," meaning the Third

World, and questioning the wisdom of overreliance on either superpower.

Now in league with several defectors from Hua's conservative group, Deng's antagonists were able to criticize his entire policy package of perceived overreliance on the United States, describing his policy toward Vietnam as abortive and one that risked war with the Soviet Union. During the next two years, Deng came under increased pressure on such issues as Taiwan and the economy, his critics citing his U.S.-oriented policy package as a caving in to U.S. interests – a policy that had not successfully furthered China's modernization needs and had delayed rather than accelerated reunification with Taiwan.

The 30-year Treaty of Friendship, Alliance, and Mutual Assistance signed in February 1950 between Beijing and Moscow officially expired in April 1980 following China's notification a year earlier of its intent to allow the treaty to end. Although the pact had been defunct for 20 years and its economic and military assistance provisions unavailable to China, it is likely that some elements in the Chinese leadership regretted its formal expiration. There is no clear indication, but it is possible that certain Chinese leaders favored renegotiation of the treaty as a balance to the new ties to the West. Those Chinese leaders seeking an officially neutralist or even independent stance may have tipped the balance by welcoming the expiration. There was some speculation at this time, at least outside China, about the possibility of the PRC joining the nonaligned movement.

But Deng was again able to obtain a consensus for his policy of détente with the United States following the December 1979 Soviet invasion of Afghanistan. The bilateral discussions with Moscow, which had begun in September 1979 in an effort to reduce internal tension and balance China's international position, were abruptly terminated. Chinese media described the international situation as a time "for action, not words," and Beijing called for a broad international anti-Soviet united front behind U.S. leadership. But subsequent events and reinterpretation of international geopolitics combined to undercut Deng's position. Following an extensive policy review, a new Chinese foreign policy orientation was officially set forth at the twelfth party congress in September 1982.

3

Underlying Principles of China's Current Policy

Policy Changes in the 1970s

The redefinition of China's international policy after 1969 brought major changes from the foreign policy positions of the 1960s. Most notable, of course, was the transfer of the title "public enemy number one" from the United States in the mid-1960s to the Soviet Union 10 years later. During the 1970s, ideology played a much less important role than in the 1960s, as China sought to build alliances with all those who opposed Soviet policies and began to advocate unity and stability rather than revolution to thwart Moscow's opportunities to advance its position.

The attention of the Chinese leadership during the first half of the 1970s was largely taken up by the internal power struggle. After the initial opening to the West, little progress was made for a number of years, although the desire to move toward a closer relationship with the capitalist world was evident. By the late 1970s, however, China's foreign policy orientation had become more clearly definable.

A strategic reassessment was made public around mid-

1978. In an application of the "encirclement" theory to the Third World, China identified three areas where it perceived a major Soviet threat: Indochina, the Middle East, and the waterways stretching from the Persian Gulf through the Indian Ocean. (According to Harry Harding of the Brookings Institution, some Chinese leaders may have taken this view considerably earlier in the decade, but were prevented by the Gang of Four's control of the press from expressing it publicly.) Rather than planning a frontal strike through Europe that would bring it into direct confrontation with the North Atlantic Treaty Organization (NATO), Moscow was now — in the PRC's analysis — engaging in a policy of strategic encirclement that would allow the USSR to gain control of the Middle East's oil fields and supply routes and achieve naval predominance in the Indian and Pacific oceans. The early 1979 overthrow of the shah and the late 1979 invasion of Afghanistan was proof for Beijing and increased Chinese accusations that Moscow was engaging in a policy of southward expansion.

During the 1970s, Africa and Latin America were also described by China as targets for Soviet hegemonistic designs, although not as immediately threatened. Beijing believed Africa was important to Moscow chiefly for its value in putting pressure on the United States, particularly in the Middle East. Latin America was also of growing interest to the Soviets, as the Chinese pointed out, because it provided opportunity for Moscow to pressure the United States in its own backyard. In both regions a Chinese drive to establish new relations and strengthen older ones reflected responses to increased Cuban and Soviet interest. Cuba and, later, Vietnam were frequently described by China as Moscow's "catspaws" and "Trojan horses" in the Third World.

Despite policy reformulation in the early 1980s, it would appear that few if any of China's major post-Cultural Revolution foreign policy trends, particularly those affecting China's

Third World relationships, will be reversed in this decade. Several, to be sure, were not actively promoted as strategic concepts at all times during the 1970s, due to emphasis on the centrality of the Sino-U.S. relationship. But the guidelines for China's current Third World policy were clearly worked out between 1970 and 1980. The following were among the most important:

Revival of the Push for Third World Leadership

Reflecting a desire both to enhance its security and independence while presenting itself as a responsible member of the international community, China formulated the Three Worlds theory in the mid-1970s. Behind the declaration of this theory as official Chinese policy lay nostalgia in some leadership quarters for the cooperative days of the late 1950s when China's position as a growing Third World power was accepted by many states and Chinese domestic and revolutionary achievements were respected. In contrast to China's position in the 1950s, however, the Five Principles of Peaceful Coexistence were now reinforced by a more specific policy formulation. Furthermore, with China's enhanced position because of its UN membership and its permanent seat on the Security Council, the PRC could aspire to influence and leadership heretofore unobtainable. The framework for China's Third World leadership drive was in place by the mid-1970s and was only delayed by internal controversy.

Renewed Interest in the Political Potential of International Organizations

Desiring to increase confidence in an independent China as a responsible global participant, the PRC joined a variety of international organizations and groupings in the 1970s, especially those affiliated with the UN. Unlike its unseemly efforts during the 1950s and 1960s to gain control over such organizations, Beijing took care to limit its role in most groups to that of observer or inactive participant. Unfamiliarity with the workings of international organizations, a desire to avoid antagonizing the Third World as in the past, and indecision at home were reflected in this new hesitancy. China did not, for example, use its UN Security Council veto even once during the 1970s.

As China's appreciation for the potential of Third World groups rose once again, it viewed Cuban efforts in the late 1970s to swing the Non-Aligned Movement toward a pro-Soviet orientation as particularly alarming, especially as China tended to regard the nonaligned countries as the core group for its own potential leadership role. Beijing feared that a pro-Soviet Non-Aligned Movement would help Vietnam consolidate its hold on Indochina and enhance Moscow's use of Cuba to influence the Third World. Despite the fact that China was eligible for membership in the movement after the 1980 expiration of the Sino-Soviet friendship treaty and a lack of moderate nonaligned leadership after the death of Tito, Beijing did not offer to join, preferring instead to retain its "independent" position while seeking to influence the course of that organization through friends such as Egypt and Pakistan. Nonetheless, the PRC's interest in Yugoslavia's use of the Non-Aligned Movement to balance East-West relations has become increasingly clear as part of an overall Chinese fascination with the Yugoslav economic and political model.

Emphasis on the Centrality of Diplomatic Ties and Declining Support for Revolutionary Armed Struggle

Beijing began returning its ambassadors to their posts in 1969 and actively sought establishment of official relations with almost all other states. Exceptions included Israel and South Africa, with whom diplomatic ties would have been opposed by the Third World. Between January 1970 and December 1980, official relations were established or resumed with 77 additional countries, most in the Third World and many desiring relations with the PRC as a direct result of Taiwan's expulsion from the UN and the PRC's accession to China's seat.

Concurrently, to reflect its new, more responsible foreign policy orientation and its desire to maintain good diplomatic ties, Beijing significantly reduced support to Third World revolutionary groups, including Communist parties. Among those no longer receiving China's support were various groups in Latin America and Africa such as the Eritrean Liberation Front, to which the PRC ceased aid in 1970 in order to establish diplomatic relations with Ethiopia. Aid to the People's Front for the Liberation of the Occupied Arab Gulf (PFLOAG) was terminated in 1973 because of opposition from Iran and from various Gulf states with which China hoped to establish ties. There was also a major cut in rhetorical support to opposition groups across the board and in aid to antigovernment Communist groups in Southeast Asia, although the PRC continued to express support for Communist internationalism and to provide low levels of aid to Communist parties in Thailand, Burma, Indonesia, the Philippines, and Malaysia.

Assistance to groups such as various Palestinian and African nationalist organizations whose objectives furthered China's Third World position continued at a moderate rate both as proof of support for Third World causes and to prevent the total reliance of such groups on the Soviet Union. Thus, Beijing continued to support liberation struggles in Africa, including the provision of military aid to several groups in southern Africa and to one faction in the mid-1970s Angolan war for independence. Support for the Palestinians, a major component in China's ties with the Arab states, began in 1964, but was influenced by the PRC's desire not to contribute to regional destabilization, thereby aiding Moscow, as well as by Beijing's recognition after 1970 that Palestinian disunity precluded transformation of the Palestinian liberation groups into an effective national liberation movement. China gradually dropped its public support for the Palestinian "armed struggle," although low levels of military aid continued, counseling the Palestinians to seek a negotiated settlement through involvement in various peace initiatives.

During the late 1970s, China faced a dilemma in seeking to maintain good relations with Egypt, which had signed a peace treaty with Israel, and with the Palestinian organizations and the other Arabs. There was grumbling on the part of some Arabs that China had betrayed its previous revolutionary spirit by providing de facto support for the Camp David efforts. Beijing, however, has long regarded close ties to Cairo as pivotal to its position in both the Middle East and Africa and managed to continue its support for Egyptian efforts to promote peaceful resolution of the Arab-Israeli dilemma while avoiding alienation of the more hardline Arab states by not openly endorsing the Camp David accords.

Redefinition of the Dictum of "Self-Reliance"

The recognition of a need to accept international assistance for China's modernization programs, including foreign investment in China, transformed the 1960s definition of self-reliance. No longer was the term to mean self-containment or refusal to participate in international programs. Under the new definition Beijing continued to warn of the dangers of allowing outside control, but counseled the Third World states to select aid carefully, with the understanding that the developed world had an obligation to assist those who had been exploited by capitalism and colonialism. This new definition appeared to promote a concept of Third World self-help and mutual support, since defined by Beijing as "collective self-reliance." In the late 1970s, self-reliance provided a convenient rationale for a major cut in China's international aid programs as China's own modernization programs were given priority.

Decline in Promotion of China as a Model for Development

Beijing's more realistic view of China's economic backwardness and the 1970s reassessment of Maoist economic policies brought about a reevaluation of China's actual position on the scale of international development. Embarrassment over the Cultural Revolution's internal economic chaos and recognition of the need for outside economic aid to achieve rapid modernization caused a decline in the vigor with which China had previously touted itself as a Third World economic role model. Beijing did not, however, cease to give advice to other Third World countries concerning application of the principle of self-reliance as demonstrated by China. This principle was, however, in changed guise.

A reassessment of the value of revolution as a foreign policy tactic and increased emphasis on formal diplomatic ties also brought an end to Beijing's major promotional campaign to cast China in the role of revolutionary model. Although Beijing did not cease to praise the values of its early revolutionary experience, this was on a much less grand scale and was constrained by the Third World's hesitation to heed a nation that had just risked self-destruction by seeking perpetual domestic revolution. Instead, a policy of "do what we advise, not as we have done" came into vogue as China began openly in the late 1970s to admit to the Cultural Revolution's "errors." The emphasis turned to China's ability to guide the Third World through application of certain aspects of China's early revolutionary experience and to help fellow Third World states learn from China's recent errors.

Renewed Efforts Toward Responsible
Regional Leadership

During the 1970s the PRC once again took up Zhou's efforts of the late 1950s to use political initiative rather than rhetoric or subversion to influence the other Asian states. Establishment of diplomatic ties with Thailand, the Philippines, Japan, and Malaysia and reduction in support for Asian Communist parties illustrated this trend, as did public recognition by China of the value of the Association of Southeast Asian Nations (ASEAN) and other regional cooperative ventures. Efforts were made as well to settle long-standing border demarcation questions with India, Burma, Nepal, and Vietnam.

The far less belligerent stance by Beijing on the Taiwan issue from the late 1970s onward relates to China's regional leadership concerns. The PRC has consistently since 1979 referred to "reunification" with Taiwan instead of "liberation," as in earlier pronouncements. Although the importance of the issue of Taiwan's reincorporation into a united China was in no way diminished, Beijing endeavored by a more moderate approach to display a spirit of cooperation and to provide the Third World, China's Asian neighbors in particular, the image of a wronged party that was nonetheless seeking to avoid precipitant action and possible regional destabilization.

China's influence in Asia was considerably extended in the 1970s through renewed or expanded cultural, economic, and political ties. As China involved itself more closely with its neighbors, its size and past position of prominence once again helped ease the reluctance of some Asian states to accept China as a regional leader. Rivalries between China and Vietnam were exacerbated, however, by China's new activism, including its military and political relations with Kampuchea. Although the close Chinese relationship with Kampuchea's Pol Pot regime was sought by Beijing to balance

Moscow's growing influence over Vietnam, Hanoi considered Kampuchea under Pol Pot a Chinese satellite.

Potential regional rivalries exist as well between China and India and between China and Japan. Although in 1972 China established diplomatic relations with Japan and restored full diplomatic ties with India (which had been disrupted in 1962), the coming years may bring increased rivalry for regional leadership between the PRC and the other two most powerful Asian states. In India in particular China faces a rival for Third World and nonaligned leadership, a competition heightened by the close Soviet-Indian relationship.

Expressions of Chinese willingness to assume a regional security role were infrequent and sometimes contradictory during the 1970s, but the PRC moved toward recognition of the need for regional security cooperation with both the United States and Japan, after the mid-1970s and toward increased activity with regard to Korea. The perception of a shifting power balance in Asia after the U.S. withdrawal from Vietnam, followed by North Vietnam's consolidation of power over the South and its subsequent invasion of Kampuchea, faced China with new regional dilemmas, as did the did the 1979 Soviet invasion of Afghanistan. China saw the Soviet Union attempting to fill a power vacuum, and, consequently, the late 1970s brought Chinese endorsements of a U.S. military role in Asia and of Japanese rearmament. Chinese support for both issues remains problematic, however. Official statements from Beijing have reflected internal debate on the extent of U.S. involvement in Asia and the possible dangers of a reborn Japanese militarism.

The 1979 Chinese invasion of Vietnam revived Asian as well as other Third World fears of a militant China. Closer ties with Thailand and most ASEAN states following the Vietnamese invasion of Kampuchea and subjugation of Laos served to repair some of the damage to China's regional image. During the late 1970s and early 1980s the PRC became more amenable to ASEAN policy initiatives on Indochina, even when Beijing did not concur in policy decisions. The PRC appeared reluctant to jeopardize newly forged diplomatic relationships with its neighbors.

Current Relations with the Third World

During the late 1970s and early 1980s Chinese foreign and domestic policies fluctuated between periods of greater openness to the West and more tightly controlled economic and social policies. Although reversion to either the extremism or the chaos of the Cultural Revolution era cannot be ruled out, the general trend continues toward stability and development. Key problems involving the economy, the military, population control, and the bureaucracy remain unresolved, however, and the end of the decade will probably find China still grappling with its age old problems of poverty, regionalism, and conservatism – all of which will affect China's relations with the Third World.

The major foreign policy trend of the early 1980s has been the Chinese effort to distance itself politically from the United States while rehabilitating its relationship with the USSR – at the same time seeking to maintain and even strengthen diplomatic and trade relations with both Washington and Moscow. This emphasis on China's independence from superpower politics and a simultaneous effort to increase Chinese influence in the Third World are consistent with China's traditional foreign policy goals.

A *Beijing Review* article of January 1984 attributes the basic principles of China's foreign policy to Mao Zedong and Zhou Enlai, describing "China's unique style of independent foreign diplomacy" and outlining "five main aspects" of present foreign relations. These are (1) independence from any big power or bloc of countries or pressure from any big nation,

(2) the development of relations with all countries on the basis of the Five Principles of Peaceful Coexistence, (3) opposition to hegemony, (4) the strengthening of unity with the Third World, and (5) the "open door," a policy of economic flexibility.

Today's policy of "independence" is indeed similar to Zhou Enlai's "neutralism" of the late 1950s, but arises from a much stronger economic motivation and is, therefore, considerably less anti-imperialist. Because China no longer has the close ties to Moscow that it had in the 1950s, the present policy is also more antihegemonist and thus is more likely to keep China independent of outside control, barring a drastic change in the international environment. Nonetheless, traditional tensions continue between various leadership elements as China seeks to strengthen itself internally and internationally. Evidence of leadership disagreement over Deng's desire for a proto-alliance with the United States surfaced sporadically in the late 1970s and early 1980s despite Chinese attempts to keep ideological debate behind closed doors. The period was one of ideological fluidity, and, despite Beijing's effort to allay foreign suspicions of growing internal division over foreign policy, such divisions became more evident in 1980, foretelling a strategic shift in the PRC's foreign relations.

Two important indicators of dissent in early 1980 were the controversial speech by Qinghua University Professor Zhang Guangdou, a copy of which was passed to a foreign correspondent in Beijing, and an article published in a Chinese provincial journal, Heilongjiang's *One Hundred Schools of Literature and Art*. Zhang's speech criticized the quality of American life, described the United States as an "imperialist" power, and said that Chinese cooperation with the United States was only of a "tactical" nature to counter the USSR. The Heilongjiang publication summarized the proceedings of a Chinese seminar on the nature of Soviet society, which concluded – in contrast to the official Chinese position – that despite Moscow's "aggressive and expansionist foreign policy. . . its domestic policy is basically socialist" and not "revisionist."

Both Zhang's speech and the Heilongjiang article reflected the growing impatience of powerful elements inside the Chinese leadership establishment with Deng's tilt toward the West. Deng fought back, punishing the Heilongjiang officials and telling a U.S. journalist that Professor Zhang had "gone haywire." Sino-U.S. relations, Deng said, "are no tactical move, no matter of expedience or short-term duration, but a major strategic decision." Nonetheless, the handwriting was on the wall, and it was not long before the Third World aspect of the impending Chinese foreign policy switch became apparent.

By late 1981 the PRC was adjusting its global posture to stress affinity with the Third World. Theoretical readjustments included revival of public discussions of the Three Worlds theory, a move toward linkage of the United States and the USSR as threats to international peace (which was clear after mid-1982), and the shift toward a more balanced stance in which the United States once again became an international "hegemonist" and there were few high level references to the USSR as "social imperialist."

Concurrently, Beijing became openly more critical of U.S. policy in the Third World, so that by early 1982 China's media were remarking on the "mistaken American policy" in the Middle East and southern Africa. Perhaps the first example of this new rhetoric was a late 1981 Chinese criticism of U.S. policy in El Salvador. In this commentary China applauded U.S. opposition to Soviet designs in the Caribbean Basin (long a Chinese theme), but questioned for the first time in several years U.S. intentions and sensitivity to local conditions.

The drive to improve the PRC's Third World credentials included a remarkable increase in high level Chinese delegations to the Third World during 1981, including three trips to Asia and one to Latin America by Premier Zhao and visits by Foreign Minister Huang Hua to Latin America, Africa, and India. At this time the Chinese also began an active program of developing party-to-party ties in the Third World, including the opening of official relations with such non-Communist ruling parties as the Iraqi Ba'th Party. Third World organizations, including the Non-Aligned Movement and the Group of 77, began to receive careful Chinese attention as part of a program to demonstrate support for Third World causes.

Two highly publicized Chinese efforts to demonstrate the PRC's influence in the Third World occurred in late 1981. At the UN China threw its support behind Tanzania's Foreign Minister Salim A. Salim in his bid to win the secretary general position from Austria's Kurt Waldheim. Although a compromise candidate was the final choice, China had, by using its Security Council veto for the first time, displayed its willingness to support Third World aspirations at the UN. The other highly visible Chinese effort was the championship of Third World economic causes at the North-South meeting of 22 world leaders in Cancun, Mexico, in October. At Cancun and at the February 1982 follow-on conference of 45 Third World nations in New Delhi, China pushed for global negotiations and the organization of South-South talks in support of Third World calls for a new international economic order.

Basic Emphases

The basic emphases of China's post-1980 foreign policy are on independence, regional influence, and the centrality of economics. Close ties with the Third World are crucial to all three, providing China with an essential international buffer against the superpowers, an expanded base for reference and authority, and even the potential for mutual economic assistance and cooperation. At the twelfth party congress, Party Chairman Hu Yaobang said, "The emergence of the

Third World on the international arena after World War II is a primary event of the time. . . . This has greatly changed the situation in which the superpowers could willfully manipulate the fate of the world."

China's independent foreign policy has meant alignment with the Third World on most policy issues. China wants to use the Third World to construct a base of influence for itself in an increasingly multipolar world. Rather than a truly neutral position between the superpowers, however, what Beijing actually seeks is the flexibility to play off the superpowers for its own benefit, and the Third World is a convenient base for this endeavor. Although Beijing is in basic agreement with the United States on the Soviet threat to world peace, China is at present working hard to avoid any position that would appear to compromise its independence. Thus the attempt by President Ronald Reagan to include China in a condemnation of Soviet global intentions during his April 1984 visit to the PRC was checked by the Chinese, who edited out the offending remarks before the president's broadcast. Furthermore, although much Chinese criticism of U.S. policy in the Third World is intended mainly to enhance the PRC's own position, China is probably sincere when it claims the root cause of the present "turbulent" world situation is U.S.-Soviet contention and insists that U.S. policies contribute to international tensions, especially in the Third World.

The desire for enhanced regional influence is the second prong of China's post-1981 foreign policy. History and specific concerns separate the PRC's Asian policy from Chinese policy elsewhere in the Third World. Latent fears of Chinese aggressiveness; competing aspirations by various states such as India, Japan, and Vietnam; and the unresolved questions of Beijing's ties to Asian Communist parties and overseas Chinese groups all complicate the issue.

China's two most immediate foreign policy problems, the future of Hong Kong and reunification with Taiwan, are Asian issues under close scrutiny by the Third World, particularly China's neighbors. Although Beijing is eager to settle the Taiwan issue and lists it as a priority problem for resolution, there is no present indication that China's current leadership will push the issue through other than diplomatic, people-to-people, and propaganda channels. Chinese sensitivity to Third World censure as well as China's regional leadership aspirations are among the factors that restrain Beijing from attempting a military reunification.

The Hong Kong issue is more immediate due to the 1997 expiration of the "unequal" treaty with Great Britain. Sino-British talks on Hong Kong began in September 1982 during Prime Minister Margaret Thatcher's visit to the PRC, and culminated in the initialing of the Sino-British joint declaration in September 1984. All signs are that Beijing hopes through the conclusion of the accord to reassure the Asian states of China's peaceful intentions, to ease apprehension in Hong Kong, and to achieve acceptance of China's position when the PRC eventually assumes sovereignty over the present British colony. Although China seeks to demonstrate to the Third World its staunchness in dealing with the imperialists, Beijing is well aware of the potential harm to its aspirations for regional influence should Hong Kong's economic infrastructure be seriously harmed.

Additionally, the PRC wishes to use a peaceful transfer of authority in Hong Kong as reassurance to the people of Taiwan. Official commitments have been made by Beijing that under PRC sovereignty the current economic systems would remain intact. According to an article of the 1982 state Constitution, Hong Kong is to be a "special administrative region" of the PRC, a promise also made to Taiwan in the 1981 peace talk proposals and since reiterated. Peaceful transfer of Hong Kong to Chinese sovereignty will thus be a prototype for a similar scenario with Taiwan, an issue of major importance for Beijing's efforts to demonstrate its restraint and fairness to the Asian Third World.

The centrality of economics in China's present foreign policy relates, of course, to the primacy of the modernization program, regarded by Beijing as crucial to China's future security, independence, and rightful international position. Placing economics rather than ideology in command has naturally strained several aspects of China's Marxist framework. Nonetheless, the ongoing economic debate inside China will likely result in continuation of current "open door" policies.

The primacy of economics puts strains on China's stated foreign policy aims as well. Desire to lead the Third World and to maintain a neutral policy toward the United States are both affected. From 1979 to 1981 China emphasized ties to the United States in order to achieve needed economic and technological assistance and cooperation and to enhance the PRC's security against the possibility of Soviet attack. Today the honeymoon is over and the PRC seeks these ends without the same close Sino-U.S. relationship (at least publicly). Furthermore, the decision to give priority to China's own economic needs brought cutbacks in China's foreign aid programs in the late 1970s, cutbacks that were not always understood and were sometimes resented by the Third World. But the post-1981 policy reform has apparently brought revision of China's Third World aid programs, as seen in a dramatic increase in China's aid after 1982.

4

China's Third World Regional Policies

In its relations with the regions of the Third World, China stresses the common experience of the struggle against imperialism, hegemonism, colonialism, and racism and the mutual interest in safeguarding national independence and developing national economies. But, according to Foreign Minister Wu Xueqian, "China is a member of the Third World, not its leader. We have never considered ourselves the leader of the Third World and will not try to be the leader in the future."

In early 1984, however, Premier Zhao observed that in the context of a "darkening volatile world situation," in which the superpowers are "scrambling for world hegemony," China offers itself as a sane leader calling for disarmament, economic redistribution, and greater power for disadvantaged nations through cooperation.

Beijing recognizes that Third World disunity, mismanagement, and exploitation by indigenous Third World leaders contribute to Third World problems, but China soft-pedals the failings of its friends, particularly in public. Overt criticism of Third World countries is almost totally restricted to actions that impinge on China's sovereignty (Vietnam) or security (Afghanistan) or, rarely, those actions that not only threaten regional destabilization but are also broadly condemned by the rest of the Third World, such as Libyan invasions of Chad. With rare exceptions, only those states China considers dominated by Moscow – Cuba, Vietnam, and Afghanistan – are publicly criticized, and even here diplomatic relations are maintained at a minimal level.

The PRC, furthermore, does not publicly differentiate among Third World states beyond the basic necessity of ascertaining whether or not the individual state is friendly to China. Whether capitalist, Communist, Arab socialist, expansionist (Libyan), dictatorial (Chile), or corrupt (Zaire), China is almost always willing to establish diplomatic ties. Even Libya's and Angola's close ties to the Soviet Union have not deterred China in recent years. The only exception to this flexibility is with regard to those states such as Israel and South Africa with whom ties would seriously harm China's relations with other Third World countries.

North Asia

As China emerges as a regional leader, its immediate neighbors are intrigued but cautious. The PRC's closest economic relationship is with Japan, upon whose support China's economic modernization programs are greatly dependent. Despite a history of antagonism, China and Japan have a natural confluence of security, economic, and political interests, which can contribute to regional stability. Since 1971 Japan has been the PRC's largest trading partner, and in 1978 the two nations signed a peace and friendship treaty.

Latent Chinese fears of Japanese militarism, unsettled territorial claims in the Senkaku Islands, the aggravation inherent in business dealings between radically opposed economic systems, and possible tensions over markets and regional leadership aspirations do not at present significantly cloud the Sino-Japanese relationship. Although it is a developed country, Japan has special Third World access due to geography, race, and economic capabilities. China hopes to use its relationship with Japan to further its economic and political position in Asia and encourages Tokyo to strengthen its ties with the Third World.

In March 1984 during a visit of Japanese Prime Minister Yasuhiro Nakasone to China, the NCNA quoted both Nakasone and the Chinese that the relationship between China and Japan is a model for countries with different social systems. The NCNA later praised Prime Minister Nakasone's May 1984 visit to Pakistan and India as "a new direction in Japan's independent and positive foreign policy."

Stability on the Korean peninsula is of considerable concern to both Beijing and Tokyo, and in 1984 both countries sought to expedite talks between the People's Democratic Republic of Korea and the Republic of Korea. Although on Indochina the views of China and Japan are virtually identical, in this case Beijing backed the North Korean proposal for tripartite talks including the United States while Tokyo favored bilateral discussions involving only the two Koreas. China irritated North Korea when the PRC failed to reject outright the U.S.-South Korea suggestion that, in addition to the United States and both Koreas, China itself be included in the discussions. It was a role Beijing would probably have welcomed but was forced to reject in face of North Korea's disapproval.

China's relations with North Korea have been generally close if not always warm during the past 30 years. Although the Chinese have a special security treaty with North Korea, Beijing has never been able to count on full cooperation or understanding from Pyongyang, which marches to the drum of its own peculiar style of Korean communism and has, moreover, a cordial relationship with Moscow toward which it can tilt if China's actions are displeasing.[30] Since the Chinese opening to the West and the normalization of its relations with the United States, Sino-Korean relations have continued their see-saw nature, but with tensions usually kept hidden. North Korea is, after all, a Chinese border state, and Beijing, which has sought to reassure Pyongyang about the Sino-U.S. relationship, desires to avoid further strains between itself and North Korea. The May 1984 visit to Pyongyang by CCP General Secretary Hu Yaobang reflected this Chinese effort.

Recent events have opened up the possibility of greater strains in Beijing's ties to Pyongyang. In early 1983 a hijacked Chinese airliner crossed unimpeded over North Korea to land in South Korea, and there is some indication Beijing may have reproached its ally for failure to take effective action that would have saved the PRC considerable international embarrassment. On the other hand, Pyongyang cannot welcome Chinese statements of support for a strong U.S. strategic presence in Asia, including implied recognition of the advisability of retention of U.S. troops in South Korea and the current linkage of withdrawal with reunification efforts. In April 1984, Beijing radio carried an analysis that appeared to praise President Reagan, who "has not only firmly cancelled the plan to withdraw U.S. troops from South Korea, but has strengthened the U.S. military presence in this region."[31] Beijing balances such statements by infrequent public chastisement of the United States for the "unwise" stationing of forces in South Korea.

North Korea is also certain to be uneasy about recent Chinese efforts to open an unofficial relationship with South Korea. In early 1984 these included increased indirect trade via Hong Kong and, in what appeared to be establishment of a new era of "sports diplomacy," the invitation of a South Korean tennis team to play a tournament in China and acceptance by China of a return invitation.[32] Several other sports exchanges have followed. In addition to increased regional leverage, China stands to benefit economically and technologically from opening an unofficial relationship with South Korea. But Beijing risks North Korean hostility over any friendly Chinese overtures toward Seoul. Moreover, if Beijing were to recognize South Korea, it would open itself to criticism that China opposes Korean unification and is prepared to pursue a "two-Korea policy" while condemning any suggestion of a "two-China policy."

Relations between the two nations may also be complicated by the recent moderation of China's international actions, while North Korea's have appeared to grow more radical. The late 1983 Rangoon bombing in which a North Korean terrorist bomb killed several high ranking members of a South Korean government delegation to Burma was deplored by Beijing — which eschews acts of international terrorism. China was restrained in its criticism of North Korea over the incident, however, probably to avoid driving Pyongyang closer to Moscow.

Southeast Asia

Southeast Asia is of importance to China for reasons of geography, economics, history, and security. To impede any further growth of Soviet influence and power, China's major policy in the region has been to limit the expansion of Vietnamese influence and to develop strong ties with the non-Communist Southeast Asian states. The close Sino-Vietnamese ties of the 1960s and early 1970s have been replaced by close Chinese cooperation with ASEAN, although the PRC has not been able to persuade two ASEAN states, Indonesia and Singapore, to establish diplomatic relations. China has growing economic ties with all Southeast Asian states with the exception of the Indochinese countries, as well as an especially cooperative relationship with Thailand because of the Vietnamese threat.

Although the three Indochinese countries – Vietnam, Kampuchea, and Laos – have officially welcomed the start of Sino-Soviet bilateral negotiations, Hanoi is concerned that any reduction of tensions between Beijing and Moscow will be to Vietnam's disadvantage. Moscow has sought to reassure Hanoi about its efforts to improve ties with Beijing, but China probably intends the Sino-Soviet talks at least in part to play on Vietnamese fears. All feelers put out by Hanoi in an effort to mend fences with China have been rejected by Beijing, which is incensed that a state that has been in China's orbit since the second century B.C. should now turn on its former mentor. Hanoi complains that "the Chinese continue to threaten us with a second lesson" (another incursion to match that of 1979), and the Vietnamese boast that, "We're a stumbling block to Chinese hegemonism and expansionism in Southeast Asia."[33]

The PRC insists on a complete Vietnamese withdrawal from Kampuchea and Laos and will continue military, propaganda, and political pressure on Vietnam until this occurs. This desire to restrain Vietnam is primarily because of Beijing's belief that Hanoi is an agent for Soviet expansionist designs, but there is also a sense in which Chinese anger with its former friend and regional subordinate (in China's view) has taken on a life of its own. A November 2, 1983, NCNA commentary referred to Vietnam as "a knife pointed by the Soviets at China" and once again demanded that the USSR stop support for Vietnamese aggression in Indochina and cease using Vietnam to threaten China and Southeast Asia. According to Beijing, "In 1983 Vietnamese troops conducted 1,000 armed provocations and opened fire at China's border areas on 650 occasions." By late spring of 1984 this situation had deteriorated even further; Vietnam was claiming limited Chinese incursions into its territory, and the most serious border clashes since 1978 had occurred.

Despite the 1982–1983 reduction of tensions between China and the Soviet Union, several basic problems remain unresolved between them. As preconditions to full normalization of relations with Moscow, Beijing demands that the Soviet Union remove three "obstacles," all of which are related to China's Third World neighbors. These are a drawdown of Soviet forces on the Chinese border and in Mongolia to pre-1965 levels, Soviet withdrawal from Afghanistan, and a halt to Soviet support for the Vietnamese occupation of Kampuchea. The strident Chinese response in April 1984 to Vietnamese incursions into Thailand and to the unprecedented joint Vietnamese-Soviet naval exercises in the Gulf of Tonkin, which included increased hostility on the Sino-Vietnamese border, illustrates continuing Chinese touchiness on the issue of Soviet support for an unfriendly and aggressive client on China's southern border.

China sees itself in a special security role vis-à-vis Thailand, although no formal security agreements have been signed. At a press conference in Bangkok in February 1981, Premier Zhao Ziyang reiterated a promise dating from the mid-1970s that if Vietnam invades Thailand, China will "resolutely stand on the side of Thailand and support the Thai people's struggle against aggression." Border clashes along the Sino-Vietnamese border in April 1984 paralleled Vietnamese military action along the Thai border. Although the Sino-Thai relationship is based on mutual security concerns, the Thai government remains strongly anti-Communist and wary of too close a relationship with the PRC. That China normalized relations with the United States, Thailand's closest ally, just prior to the Vietnamese invasion of Kampuchea in 1979, however, probably facilitated the new Sino-Thai relationship.

Although China provides aid to the Khmer Rouge, which

it believes is the only really effective force fighting against the Vietnamese occupation of Kampuchea, Beijing also supports the non-Communist resistance and would almost certainly prefer Prince Sihanouk as head of a coalition government to a return to power of former Kampuchean leader Pol Pot. China fears that the ASEAN states will not persist in their anti-Vietnamese resolve and seeks to bolster their determination. Nonetheless, the Third World has criticized continuing Chinese support for Pol Pot, and China has sought to reassure the Southeast Asian nations that it favors a nonaligned Kampuchea.

The PRC's relations with the non-Communist Southeast Asian states have continued to improve in recent years despite unresolved problems. Overseas Chinese populations are regarded with suspicion in several Southeast Asian countries, and in early 1984 during Foreign Minister Wu's visit to Kuala Lumpur, Malaysia, Beijing stated it would not issue special visas to Malaysian Chinese, thus enabling them to circumvent Kuala Lumpur's regulations against travel to that country. The other major irritant in Chinese ties with Southeast Asia is the lingering Chinese relationship with regional Communist parties. The evolution of a close Sino-Thai relationship since 1980 has caused Beijing to cut back and perhaps eliminate altogether its support for the Thai Communist Party. Nonetheless, at least low levels of Chinese aid and moral support probably continues to regional Communist parties, including those of Burma, Malaysia, and Indonesia.

South Asia

During the late 1970s, Beijing frequently described the land bridge from India westward to Turkey as a critical Soviet target in Moscow's southward push. The Soviet invasion of Afghanistan in 1979 appeared to justify China's foreboding, but as the Soviets have not invaded either Pakistan or Iran, Beijing has seen some benefit in having Soviet forces bogged down in Afghanistan. Although China initially favored a united international military response to the Soviet invasion, it now supports the negotiated settlement favored by Pakistan while it continues to provide some support to the Afghan resistance groups and calls for an unconditional Soviet withdrawal from Afghanistan.

For the PRC, Pakistan is a major buffer between China's western provinces and the possibility of Soviet encroachment. After 1979, military agreements between Islamabad and Washington resulting from the Soviet invasion of Afghanistan removed China as Pakistan's chief military supplier. But a close military, economic, and political relationship continues. In past years China has used Pakistan's good offices to ameliorate tensions with other countries, including Iran and the United States. Pakistan is a leader in the Islamic Conference Organization and the Non-Aligned Movement as well as in the United Nations, and it is likely that Beijing, which supports Islamabad in its pro-Islamic and anti-Soviet regional politics, expects to continue to use its ties to Pakistan to strengthen relations with international and nonaligned groups.

Although the Sino-Pakistani relationship evolved in part from a desire to thwart India's regional advantage, China is eager to improve relations with New Delhi and has since 1981 conducted periodic talks aimed at resolving their border controversy. Huang Hua's June 1981 trip to India was the first by a high ranking Chinese official since Zhou Enlai's visit in 1960. But the Sino-Indian relationship continues to be haunted by China's military supply relationships with both Bangladesh and Pakistan, New Delhi's own relations with Moscow, mutual suspicion, and conflicting regional aspirations.

The Soviet invasion of Afghanistan, which led to a close U.S.-Pakistani military bond, consequently allowed Moscow to strengthen its ties to New Delhi, a source of considerable apprehension in Beijing. Another source of friction is the Sino-Indian rivalry for influence in the Third World, as well as competition for concessionary loans and international markets. Prime Minister Indira Gandhi reflected this tension in a January 1984 Associated Press interview in which she claimed that the U.S. decision to reduce its contributions to the international credit institutions would be a major hurdle in Indo-U.S. relations and asserted that because "China is now a member of the International Development Association, the amount available has to be divided and, hence, it is India's assistance that is cut."

The Middle East and North Africa

Diplomatic relations with Egypt, Syria, Iran, and Morocco were among China's first Third World ties. Since the Cultural Revolution, official relations have been established with all Middle Eastern states except Israel, Bahrain, Qatar, and Saudi Arabia. China's strong interest in the region reflects recognition of the area's potential for igniting a superpower conflict as well as the hope of achieving additional Third World leverage through endorsement of Arab causes.

Beginning in 1982, the Middle East and Central America joined southern Africa and Taiwan as focal points for Chinese attacks on the United States for its efforts to assert hegemony. Beijing no longer portrays U.S. and Chinese interests as parallel in the Middle East. In mid-1982, for the first time in several years, China directly denounced U.S. mediation efforts in the region. Another change in China's Middle East policy has been a growing flexibility with regard to diplomatic relations. In the past, fear of the destabilizing effects of both Islamic fundamentalism and political extremism caused

China to emphasize its ties to the more politically conservative Arab states such as Egypt, Jordan, and Morocco. Since
1981, however, Beijing has moved to improve ties with Libya,
Iraq, Iran, and South Yemen in an effort to compete more
effectively with Moscow.[34] One other policy initiative since
1980 has been the Chinese attempt to use Islam as a political
tool, concentrated on the heavily Islamic Middle East and
South Asia — a policy reminiscent of Beijing's attempts during the 1950s to emphasize China's Islamic sympathies.

China's major concerns in the Middle East are those that
concern most nations: the continuing Arab-Israeli dilemma,
the Iran-Iraq war, the Lebanese disaster, and security in the
Gulf. But all of these conflicts are now described in official
Chinese statements as having in some way resulted from the
superpowers' contention for regional control. Although China
has at present little real clout in the Middle East, Beijing
seeks to emphasize its interest in the region and to encourage
Arab acceptance of China's growing Third World role. Following an early 1984 visit to Iraq, Kuwait, Jordan, and Egypt,
National People's Congress Standing Committee Vice Chairman Wang Renzhong said that the leaders of those four Arab
countries "trusted China fully" and "strongly desired to promote relations with China," whereas China "appreciated the
four countries' efforts to pursue a policy of independence, self-
determination and non-alignment," exactly the goals China
claims for itself.

The PLO, one of China's few avenues for direct involvement in the Middle East, has been severely damaged by the
Lebanese war. Nonetheless, Beijing continues to honor the
PLO's aid requests and to give rhetorical support to PLO
leader Yasir Arafat, who once again visited the PRC in May
1984 and was received with the ceremony due a visiting head
of state. Although China may perceive some value in Israel's
anti-Soviet position in the Middle East, this value is more
than countered in Beijing's analysis by the turmoil and con-

sequent opportunities for the Soviets that Israel's behavior causes.

Beijing no longer insists upon an Israeli withdrawal from Arab areas occupied before 1967, and, in contrast to earlier years, China has said publicly since 1979 that Israel has a right to exist as a state. But Beijing does continue to call for a Palestinian homeland and to denounce Zionism as an extension of U.S. policy. According to CCP leader Hu Yaobang in late 1982, "the disastrous effects of Israeli aggression and expansion must be eliminated and the national rights and dignity of the Palestinian people restored, while recognizing the Israeli people's right to peaceful existence." He added that "the Chinese government holds that Israel's ferocity in committing aggression is directly connected with the United States' connivance and support."

Beijing seeks to encourage regional policies that limit Soviet involvement and, therefore, encourages indigenous problem-solving through negotiations. The roles played by Syria and Libya in Lebanon have distressed China, which for years has extolled Arab unity as the only way to thwart Soviet intention. China fears that Moscow will gain greater control over the radical Arabs, and in February 1984 the Chinese news agency suggested that the United States participate in "serious talks" with Syria. Although a Syrian-Lebanese solution would be best in China's view, clearly Beijing favors a U.S.-Syrian dialogue that could cut out the Soviets.

High level visits between Chinese and Middle Eastern leaders are frequent and included a September 1983 visit to the PRC by Jordan's King Hussein, the king's second visit to China in one year. Hussein's previous visit, in December 1982, was as head of an Arab League delegation that treated China as a great power by presenting to it an Arab peace plan for the Middle East. Establishment of diplomatic relations between the PRC and Jordan in 1977 illustrated the moderation and pragmatism of post-Cultural Revolution politics. In previous years, China had frequently pledged to the PLO that it would regard Jordan exactly as it did "the Zionist entity."

China would like to function as a mediator of Arab differences, but finds itself too much an outsider to attempt such a role, except possibly through the United Nations. The PRC has, in fact, chosen this avenue to begin to take a more active part in international efforts to resolve the Middle East dilemma. Chinese representatives began to attend meetings of the UN Interim Force in Lebanon (UNIFIL) regularly in 1981, and China was represented at the vice ministerial level at UN-sponsored talks on Palestine in Geneva in 1983. Beijing's endorsement in early 1984 of the thirty-eighth UN General Assembly's resolution calling for convening of an international peace conference on the Middle East reflects an increased Chinese willingness to participate in efforts to move toward peace in the region.

Another Middle Eastern nation, Turkey, is also a member of NATO, and it is seen by China as the Third World's strongest bulwark on the southern flank of the Soviet Union. Beijing worries about instability and Soviet-sponsored unrest in Turkey and has warned Ankara to be vigilant. In early 1984, China and Turkey agreed to hold discussions on economic, trade, industrial, scentific, and technological cooperation to augment their already friendly relations. President Li Xiannian visited Turkey in 1984 and undoubtedly used the occasion to emphasize China's support for such Third World "Islamic" issues as the Palestinian question and the Afghan resistance movement.

Africa

The PRC continues to strengthen its position in Africa and now has diplomatic relations with all African states except Swaziland, Malawi, and South Africa. In 1983 Beijing established diplomatic relations with Angola, the Ivory Coast, and Lesotho and also developed contacts with Malawi and Swaziland. As well as an arena in which to thwart Soviet influence, Africa is important to the PRC as an outlet for Chinese exports and labor and because it provides an opportunity to polish China's credentials as a Third World leader.

Following the Cultural Revolution, China maintained a low profile in Africa until approximately 1978. As the decade ended, however, Chinese uneasiness over increasing Soviet and Cuban influence as a result of events in Angola in 1975 and in the Horn in 1977 precipitated a more active Chinese role. Foreign Minister Huang Hua visited Zaire in June 1978, signaling the beginning of increased Chinese activity on the continent.

From 1981-1984, China concentrated its policy initiatives on the southern African states in an effort to counter Soviet dominance in Angola, Zambia, and Mozambique. As a corollary to countering the superpowers, another basic thrust of China's African policy has been to seek prestige by presenting itself as mentor and moral leader in the Third World's struggle for economic development and national independence. From the early 1970s on, Chinese goals in Africa have paralleled those of the United States – political stability, negotiated settlements, and economic development. Nonetheless, even before its 1981 policy reformulation, the PRC sought to exploit anti-U.S. sentiment in Africa. After 1981, there was increased criticism of U.S. policy, particularly of the U.S. relationship with South Africa.

China has consistently endorsed the position of the black African states, which seek to isolate South Africa politically and economically. Beijing accuses South Africa of a domestic policy of "barbaric racism" and a foreign policy that promotes regional instability. Along with black African nations, Beijing opposes the linking of the withdrawal of Cuban troops from Angola with Namibian independence by the United

States, arguing that the United States should confront South African apartheid more directly. By early 1984 Beijing professed to see the emergence of "a trend toward a political solution" in southern Africa and had favorably publicized the U.S. role in promoting peace in the region. But in other commentaries, Beijing expressed doubt that the United States and the USSR would "cease to interfere" in southern Africa, questioned whether South Africa would keep its agreements with Angola and Mozambique, and termed the U.S. role self-serving.

Despite the problems China faced in Africa during the 1960s, nearly 30 years of military and economic assistance to Africa has generally paid off for China in a reputation for fairness and generosity. But Moscow's increased interest in Sub-Saharan Africa in the 1970s, which included large-scale arms promises – as well as U.S. and Western European economic assistance programs – have placed Beijing at a disadvantage. Where military needs were foremost, as in the Horn and in the struggle against Rhodesia, China lost out to Soviet influence. Beijing instead responded with a modified aid program to a variety of African states. Since the late 1970s, however, China has demonstrated growing interest in arms sales both for reasons of foreign exchange and to maintain contact with a variety of governments. From 1982–1984 Africa has been the focus of a dramatic upswing in Chinese military and economic aid projects to the Third World. Major recipients have been Zambia, Tanzania, and Zaire.

China's closest friends in Africa include Somalia (at the expense of its ties to Ethiopia) and Sudan (dating from the abortive 1971 Soviet-sponsored coup attempt against President Gafar Mohamed Nimeiri). The PRC also has close ties to Botswana as the result of a particularly generous aid program, to Congo (Brazzaville) despite that state's support for the Soviets on several regional and international issues, and to Zimbabwe as a result of pre-independence Chinese aid to Prime Minister Robert Mugabe's Zimbabwe African National Union (ZANU). In the early 1980s, China has shown greater willingness to conduct normal relations with African states and groups that have strong Soviet ties. The intention is to prevent total reliance on the USSR and to cause, if possible, a weakening of ties to Moscow.

The PRC maintains ties with several liberation groups in Africa to which arms are donated rather than sold. Although China advocates negotiated settlements for regional problems, Beijing also advocates armed struggle against South Africa. Groups that have a China connection include the Southwest Africa People's Organization (SWAPO) in Namibia (SWAPO leader Sam Nujoma visited China in 1983) and both the Pan Africanist Congress and the African National Congress. China has urged the latter two groups to unite their efforts against South Africa.

China's major pre-independence support to Mugabe has strengthened China's relations with Zimbabwe. In that struggle, China, unlike the Soviet Union, backed the winning contestant, but was not so fortunate in Angola where pre-independence Chinese support for the National Union for the Total Independence of Angola (UNITA) caused the victorious Popular Movement for the Liberation of Angola (MPLA) to scorn ties with the PRC for a number of years after 1975. Beijing also provided significant aid to the Front for the Liberation of Mozambique (FRELIMO) before Mozambique's independence, although Moscow's ability to provide greater quantities of aid undercut Chinese influence even before FRELIMO's 1975 victory.

A strenuous effort has been made by China not to repeat the errors of the 1960s, and Beijing has consequently sought to avoid arming black Africans against black Africans. Nonetheless, a desire to stop the Soviets has several times put

China into potentially compromising positions, such as in the arming of anti-MPLA forces in Angola in 1975, of Zaire against anti-Mobutu invaders from Angola in 1977–1978, and of Somalia against Ethiopia from 1978 on. Such arms supplies have been open, however, and Beijing is not thought to be involved in any covert efforts to overthrow black African governments.

Beginning in the late 1970s, the PRC has also encouraged more active Second and Third World roles in Africa as a show of unity against the superpowers. Examples include verbal support for the Saudi's backing of Somalia in the 1977 Ogaden war and for Moroccan and Belgian help for Zaire in 1978. Beijing now suggests to African states that economic aid be sought from Western Europe rather than from the USSR or even from the United States.

The obstacles Beijing faces to African acceptance of China's Third World leadership ambitions are evident. China lacks economic leverage in a region where development is the primary concern. The Sino-Soviet rivalry for influence has also had an effect on China's relations with several African states including Ethiopia, Madagascar, and Mozambique. Minor problems include some lingering fears of Chinese radicalism because of China's imprudence in the 1960s and concern about Chinese racism following several racially inspired incidents involving African students in China in the early 1980s.

China does, however, have political clout in Africa, and increased Chinese use of international forums will allow greater Chinese leverage in Africa in the coming years. Premier Zhao Ziyang's December 1982–January 1983 visit to 11 African countries and the visits to China of the presidents or prime ministers of at least a dozen African countries in 1983 and the first half of 1984 underscored the importance China ascribes to relations with this segment of the Third World.

Latin America

During the past two years China has become even more concerned about events in Latin America than in Africa. This
change has come about as increased turbulence in Central
America in particular has aroused greater international attention and closer involvement by both the United States and
the USSR. In February 1984, China had diplomatic relations
with 15 Latin American countries and, according to Beijing,
trade links "with more than 30 countries and regions on that
continent."

As developing countries, most Latin American states
have little to offer to China technologically. But the PRC has
expanding trade ties, including trade agreements, with several Latin countries for the importation of raw materials (including significant amounts of copper from Chile) and the
export of light industrial products. The PRC maintains membership in an increasing variety of international groups that
meet in or relate to Latin America, allowing expansion of
cultural, educational, agricultural, scientific, and other ties,
and Chinese scientists have participated in three expeditions
to the South Pole since 1980 in cooperation with Chilean expeditions. Certain Latin American countries are, moreover,
more advanced than other parts of the Third World and can
offer access to technology. There is, for example, Chinese
interest in cooperating with Mexico in petroleum production.

Ten South and Central American states maintain official
relations with Taiwan, and Beijing is interested in undercutting Taiwan in its last diplomatic stronghold. In the nearby
Caribbean, another area of Beijing-Taipei rivalry, the PRC
and Taiwan are each recognized by five countries. Taipei has
enhanced its position in the Caribbean through economic and
technological assistance, but Beijing has virtually no aid arrangements with Latin America other than having given
minimal aid to Jamaica in the 1970s.

The 1981 change in Chinese policy brought a sharp up-swing in China's attacks on U.S. policy in Latin America, as elsewhere in the Third World. Paradoxically, Beijing now criticizes Washington for too aggressive a Latin American policy, whereas previously the United States was accused of caving in to Soviet pressures. The Chinese dilemma – seeking to encourage a strong U.S. response to the Soviet presence in the U.S. backyard, but fearing U.S. domination of these Third World countries – is evident in China's treatment of the U.S. invasion of Grenada in late 1983. The NCNA described the act as "a naked, bloody aggression," and said "speculations are running high on who will be the next target."[35]

Subsequent Chinese press commentary concluded that, "although the U.S. armed invasion of Grenada played a certain role in restraining the infiltration of the other super-power, yet it aggravated the war crisis in this region and was opposed by the governments and people of various Latin American countries." The most revealing part of this comment is probably the final phrase. Beijing hopes to align with Third World thinking as closely as possible, often waiting until the majority viewpoint becomes clear before giving China's official position.

Such hesitation was displayed in China's reaction to the Argentinian occupation of the Falkland Islands in early 1982. There, the Chinese devotion to the principles of self-deter-mination and nonaggression ran athwart what many Latin American states believed to be an issue of national sovereign-ty. The Chinese made no statement on the Argentine inva-sion for several days, although Beijing eventually gave public support to Argentina. Nevertheless, Beijing sought a low pro-file on the issue, urged a negotiated settlement, and abstained on the British resolution at the UN.

In a political analysis of the causes of instability in Latin America, *People's Daily* said recently that, "the Reagan admin-istration has realized that . . . the root cause of the long-term instability in Central America . . . lies in the social contradictions of the Central American countries. . . . both military measures and pacificatory measures of reform are necessary." This is a remarkable statement from a country that for nearly 20 years had blamed most international problems on the machinations of the superpowers – and continues to do so at least publicly in other areas of the world. But the continuing Chinese ambivalence over the causes of Latin American unrest and China's desire to gain the favor of Third World countries is reflected later in the same commentary. In apparent contradiction to the earlier statement, *People's Daily* criticized the United States for "a high-handed policy toward the Nicaraguan government and people" and concluded that "facts have proved that the interference by external forces is the main reason for the instability and disturbances in Central America."

A major theme that China underlines in its dealings with the Third World, including Latin America, is the need for indigenous solutions to problems. The signing by Argentina and Chile in early 1984 of a draft treaty aimed at solving the Beagle Channel controversy was hailed by Beijing as "the first important result obtained by two neighboring countries in South America in settling a dispute over territory." China supports and frequently praises peace efforts by the Contadora group of Latin American countries, contrasting these efforts with the role of the United States, which "has unceasingly intensified its intervention activities in this region."

It is probably not just Soviet-sponsored unrest in Latin America and the possibility that U.S. action could further Soviet advantage that China fears. What would be more serious would be an undercutting of China's potential leadership by the resurgence of U.S. interest in the area. The number of Latin American countries and the issues in which Latin countries are involved make the region a natural one for Chinese attention. China has expressed concern about the possibility of nuclear proliferation in Latin America and backs the position of some Latin states that importing of nuclear weapons into the region should be prohibited. Latin America is, moreover, crucial to Chinese efforts to identify itself with Third World positions on Law of the Sea and a new international economic order. According to the NCNA in February 1984, the vice chairman of the National People's Congress Foreign Affairs Committee reaffirmed "that China's foreign policy stresses strengthening relations with Latin American countries." He is certain that "new progress will be made in cooperative links between China and Latin America."

5

Points of Contact
with the Third World

China's ability to identify itself with Third World causes is a useful counter to other aspects of China's international policy that have little appeal for the Third World. The current Chinese desire to contain Soviet expansionism is, for example, hardly more attractive to some segments of the Third World than were Chinese efforts in the 1960s to enlist the Third World in anti-Soviet and anti-U.S. organizations. Nor is Beijing's role in the Sino-Soviet-U.S. triangle a point of identification with the Third World. Although developing countries may admire the PRC's clout with the superpowers, the relationship points up the differences between China and the rest of the Third World and raises questions regarding whether or not China, because of its size and international position, is truly a Third World member.

Third World Issues

Championship of Third World causes is, therefore, an important Chinese lever for achieving Third World influence. Statements from Beijing relating to the Third World are often coupled with reminders that China, a Third World country, opposes the present international system in which the Third World remains oppressed. Such rhetoric includes support for Third World positions on disarmament, nuclear free zones and zones of peace, technology transfers, Law of the Sea, and a new international economic order, as well as efforts to address problems such as population control and economic aid from the perspective of the developing world.[36]

Disarmament

The PRC position on both conventional and nuclear disarmament is essentially that it is the duty of the superpowers to disarm first and, while they delay doing so, the Third World is at liberty to continue to arm itself. At the UN, China's voting record on disarmament is the one area in which it has not invariably sided with the Third World. Rather, the Chinese vote has frequently been determined by the position taken by the USSR, whose repeated calls for a world disarmament conference China has through the years termed a hoax.

Although Third World countries usually support disarmament proposals, China has often opposed them or withheld its vote to express disapproval. Foreign Minister Huang Hua's mid-1979 address to the General Assembly Special Session on Disarmament – the first appearance of a PRC delegation at a disarmament conference – was an attempt to justify China's voting record on disarmament to the Third World. China's attendance itself probably reflected Third World pressure. Five years later, although Beijing continues to warn that the superpowers are not sincere in attempts to reach agreement on disarmament procedures, there are indications that China will take a more active role – possibly as a Third World spokesman – in international attempts to encourage disarmament.

Nuclear Power

China's position as a Third World nuclear power remains of particular interest to all countries. In 1964 when China exploded its first nuclear device, some Third World states welcomed the event, believing China had "broken the color bar." Being a member of the exclusive nuclear club raised China's prestige but also pressured Beijing to share its technology with other developing countries. Although not a signatory of the Nuclear Non-Proliferation Treaty, the PRC fears nuclear proliferation, and Beijing today claims that China, "has always stood for the complete prohibition and thorough destruction of nuclear weapons." Nonetheless, the PRC has been accused of sale of nuclear-related technology to both Pakistan and Argentina.

For several years China rejected any type of international inspection of its nuclear facilities, but has recently agreed to certain safeguards and supervisory measures in order to have access to nuclear technology from the United States and Japan. In 1984 China joined the International Atomic Energy Agency and, for the first time, attended in observer status a meeting of the International Maritime Organization convened to discuss the dumping of nuclear waste. This more mature Chinese approach to nuclear issues is likely to be reassuring to the nuclear powers as well as to many of China's Third World friends.

Law of the Sea

China uses its support for the Law of the Sea convention, passed in 1982, as a device to oppose the superpowers. Although China itself adheres to a 12-mile limit, it says coastal states should have the right to determine an "exclusive economic zone" of from 12 to 200 nautical miles. In March 1982 China supported the Group of 77's rejection of proposed U.S.

amendments to the draft Law of the Sea document. China backs the Third World in Law of the Sea matters to support Latin American efforts to win international acceptance of a 200-nautical mile territorial sea. But endorsement of Third World positions on national boundaries and maritime resources serves as well to protect China's own wealthy coastal area.

Technology Transfer

China's position on technology transfer is that industrialized countries should give up their "monopoly" on science and technology. To this end China advocates generous developed country assistance and concessionary terms for the developing world. Aid is a "duty" for those who are better off and even a compensation for past injustices. Such a position is, of course, complementary to China's own modernization needs.

New International Economic Order

The theory of contradictions that allows for simultaneous application of opposing principles can be seen at work in China's support of technology transfer to the Third World, as well as in Beijing's support for a new international economic order. China's recognition of "contradictions" allows knowledge sharing and the acceptance of external aid in tandem with its adherence to the basic principle of self-reliance. The PRC continues its verbal support for a new international economic order although China has been disappointed in the past by the inability of the less developed countries (LDCs) to achieve a unified position on the issue. Typically, after the February 1982 conference in New Delhi, China blamed the Third World's failure to move toward South-South negotiations in order to pressure the developing world on U.S. unwillingness to be more "sincere" and forthcoming in efforts to assist Third

World developments. Essentially, however, Chinese efforts to promote a new international economic order are sincere and are geared more toward compromise than confrontation.

In the mid-1970s China praised use of "the oil weapon" by Third World countries, particularly the Arab states, against the West. Although Beijing no longer openly advocates the manipulation of the petroleum supply to threaten the developed world, it does encourage greater South-South economic cooperation as a means to break "the imperialist monopoly over international finance," enabling Third World countries to "play a positive role in the struggle . . . to establish a new economic order." A February 1984 *People's Daily* commentary praises various Arab organizations for rechanneling petrodollars to the Third World, but points out that the return of most petrodollars to the capitalist West is not altogether bad because "the inflow of petrodollars to the West constitutes a strong lever . . . [for] the oil producing countries to exert economic influence over the West."

International Organizations

In addition to adopting Third World positions on various functional issues, Beijing also has access to a variety of more tangible levers that it can manipulate in an effort to increase its Third World position. One of these is support for and membership in international organizations, including those of the Third World. The number of international groups in which China is a member, particularly those that concentrate on issues of interest to the Third World, has jumped since 1980 – as has the level of Chinese involvement in these groups.

From the standpoint of China's Third World aspirations, the UN remains the most effective international organization, and the PRC is a member of most of the UN-associated intergovernmental agencies. UN membership is beneficial to China for more than just the international recognition it receives. Among the financial benefits has been the $50 million bequest made to the PRC by the UN Fund for Population Activities for 1980–1984, which is up for renewal for 1985–1989. UN membership also provides China contact with states with which it has no official relations and access to UN groups such as the International Labor Organization and the UN Educational, Scientific, and Cultural Organization (UNESCO) in which China fears Soviet influence is too strong. In past years the PRC has used the UN and its constituent organizations to conduct economic as well as political business with countries such as South Korea, Saudi Arabia, and Israel.

When the PRC joined the UN, some Third World countries anticipated immediate Chinese influence over measures relevant to the Third World. The Palestinians, for example, felt that, "Having China on the Security Council will be like having a Palestinian there." For reasons of its own, chiefly caution with regard to an unfamiliar institution and political disagreement at home, China did not live up to these expectations. For several years, nonparticipation was the Chinese device for reconciling its "principled stand" with the desires of its Third World friends.

But China is very sensitive to Third World issues at the UN, and its voting record shows the PRC to be increasingly influenced by pressures from the Third World. It was certainly due in part to the request of various of its Third World colleagues that China abstained on the Security Council resolution condemning the Soviet Union for shooting down a South Korean airliner in late 1983.[37] In the 19 other Security Council resolutions of 1983, China voted with the United States. In the General Assembly, however, China's vote aligns the PRC with the Third World mainstream, with the PRC voting against the United States almost 80 percent of the time in 1983. This voting record is a fascinating illustration of the conflict China faces as an emerging power with global responsibilities, but one that still desires to portray itself as a member of the developing world.

The UN General Assembly and its constituent organizations also provide China a convenient forum in which to seek Third World favor by condemning both the United States and the USSR for their faults and evil intentions. Washington's announcement in late 1983 that the United States would withdraw from UNESCO in one year was "regretted" by Beijing, which then proceeded to condemn both Washington and Moscow for their attitudes toward UNESCO. An article in China's authoritative *Shijie Zhishi* (World Knowledge) said that the growth of Third World strength had gradually enabled UNESCO to break free of manipulation by the big powers, and a major cause of the U.S. decision to leave UNESCO was simply its disgruntlement over being placed at a disadvantage in the organization. Another factor, according to the Chinese publication, is superpower rivalry inside UNESCO, as "the Soviet Union is making use of the contradiction between the U.S. and the Third World to expand its influence in the organization under the guise of supporting the Third World and to isolate and attack the U.S. in various activities of the organization."

Access to the UN as a forum is of particular importance to Beijing, as China, unlike the Soviet Union, does not have membership in a broad network of international Communist front organizations. Although China was once a member of groups such as the AAPSO, the International Organization of Journalists, the World Peace Council, and the International Union of Students, ties were broken years ago as a result of the Sino-Soviet split—in some cases before such groups evolved into Communist front organizations.

Since 1980 China has displayed increased willingness to deal at least informally with countries of all political stripes, be they Soviet clients or capitalist dictatorships. This flexibility is reflected in its expanding participation and membership in international groups. China has been welcomed into organizations ranging from the International Red Cross and the World Jurist Conference to the Asian Forum of Parliamentarians on Population and Development. In March 1984 the PRC sent its first delegation to the Interparliamentary Union where the Chinese were informed they had been "expected for 30 years." In April 1984 a representative of the All-China Federation of Trade Unions attended an international meeting of trade union leaders in Nicaragua.

Nonetheless, lack of Chinese membership in the Third World's two major non-UN organizations, the Group of 77 and the Non-Aligned Movement, probably reduces Chinese effectiveness in influencing Third World countries. Although eligible to join both organizations, China remains reluctant, partly because of the history of Sino-Soviet rivalry for control of Third World groups. More important, however, is that China's failure to join the major Third World groups probably is the best available proof that China truly seeks independence, not neutrality. To join the politically-oriented Third World organizations risks impinging on China's freedom of action. From the outside, nonetheless, Beijing contests Moscow's claim that the USSR is the "natural ally" of the Non-Aligned Movement and seeks to use its friends inside the movement to counter Soviet efforts to bring that organization under Moscow's influence.

China also encourages Third World cooperation and mutual support through international organizations that China is ineligible to join. Major examples are the Organization of African Unity, the Arab League, ASEAN, the Islamic Conference Organization, and a myriad of smaller groups geared toward economic, journalistic, educational, scientific, and other exchanges. The PRC does not provide strong verbal support to the Organization of American States, whose independence is questioned by China because it is headquartered in Washington and supported by the United States.

But there are some groups in which the PRC's membership or nonmembership has caused considerable controversy.
The International Atomic Energy Association is one such.
In 1984 India threatened to leave the organization when the
PRC was granted board membership, fearing India might be
downgraded from its position as one of the association's gov-
ernors. The controversy caused some embarrassment among
Third World countries—which feared they would be called
upon publicly to support one side or the other—until the issue was resolved by allowing both China and India to sit on
the board.

In mid-1984 China appeared to be moving toward joining
the General Agreement on Tariffs and Trade (GATT), membership in which would more closely integrate the PRC into
the international economic system. But fears have been expressed in the Third World that China's membership will
bring complications and possible revision of the U.S. duty
free programs for LDCs. It was not until the late 1970s that
China began to seek financial aid in the form of grants and
concessional loans from non-Communist governments and
international financial institutions, and the first concrete
signs of the Chinese redefinition of its policy of self-reliance
came in its request for $100 million in aid from the UN
Development Program in late 1978. In 1979 the PRC accepted U.S. credits of $2 billion over a five year period and
began to receive direct commercial loans on the international
market. Since then the PRC has joined the World Bank, the
International Monetary Fund, the International Development
Association, and the International Financial Corporation.

Chinese funding from and involvement in international
financial institutions is expected to climb during the 1980s
and will inevitably create competition with other Third World
states for available development monies. According to the
NCNA, by the end of 1983 the PRC had used $468 million
in foreign funds to develop its agricultural programs. These

funds were obtained through the UN Food and Agricultural Organization, the World Grain Program, the UN Development Program, the International Agricultural Development Fund, the World Bank, and several Second World countries. India's negative reaction to China's membership in the International Development Association (as recounted in chapter 4) is prophetic.

Even more controversial is the PRC's application for membership in groups such as the Asian Development Bank, of which Taiwan is a founding member. Nonetheless, although Beijing demands membership as the representative of China, it does not oppose Taiwan's continued participation in some form, and discussions are going on to discover a formula acceptable to all parties. China's nonconfrontational approach is illustrated by the fact that its announcement of intention to join the bank was made in late 1982.

Aid and Trade

Other levers to Chinese influence in the Third World are aid and trade. Since the 1950s China has used both as avenues to contact and influence developing nations. Hoping to enhance its image and to compete for economic and political advantage in the developing world, China began a foreign aid program in 1956 – a remarkable undertaking for a state as poor and underdeveloped as China was at that time. Loans were typically for small projects and repayable with extremely low interest and over long periods. Arms were never sold but always donated, a policy that was not reversed until 1979 under the pressure of increased need for foreign exchange and less need for international revolution. Until then Beijing had frequently proclaimed that "China will never become an arms merchant."

Despite the Chinese claim, it is incorrect to characterize

Chinese aid as disinterested or "without strings" – either in the past or at present. During the late 1950s and through the 1960s, Chinese aid was clearly intended to assist the rise to power of Maoist-style leaders and to enhance the possibility for successful armed struggle against the superpowers. After years of internal struggle, the Chinese leaders today are not quite so ambitious. But the basic objective remains: the building of Chinese influence in the Third World at the expense of the superpowers.

A significant feature of the Chinese foreign aid program through the years has been China's ability to continue aid even when the recipient government has become increasingly hostile – for example, in various African countries in the early 1960s and in the People's Democratic Republic of Yemen and Afghanistan during the late 1970s. Such perseverence has arisen from desire to counter growing Soviet influence and is more typical of the response of a great power than that of a developing nation.

China's foreign aid program totaled less than $30 million annually through 1959, with the entire amount going to Cambodia, Ceylon, Indonesia, Nepal, the United Arab Republic, and Yemen. But after 1960 Chinese aid increased to some $125 million per year to more than 20 nations in Asia, Africa, and the Middle East.[38] By 1970 China had provided almost $700 million in economic assistance programs to developing countries, a rate that continued to climb until 1977 when internal domestic needs and a refocusing of foreign policy priorities caused an approximately 50 percent reduction.

China's aid programs, however, are currently in the process of an intriguing transformation, and there has been a significant increase in Chinese aid – both economic and military – to the LDCs during 1983 and 1984. From 1982 to 1983 China's military aid agreements with the developing world nearly tripled, while preliminary figures for economic aid programs to LDCs for the same period indicate a jump from $40 million to $230 million. These new commitments appear to employ fewer concessionary terms, such as grant aid and interest free loans, than in the past.

According to the NCNA, "the essential point is encouragement of reciprocal economic cooperation rather than one-way assistance." But the PRC has definitely adopted an aid program to suit its new search for Third World influence. During his 1983 visit to 11 African countries, Premier Zhao Ziyang stressed four principles for economic relationships between the PRC and other Third World countries: equality and mutual benefit, stress on actual results, use of varied forms, and common development.

Speaking to the 1982 twelfth party congress, Hu Yaobang foreshadowed the present policy by saying that, "Whether in providing aid or co-operation for mutual benefit, China has always strictly respected the sovereignty of the other party, attaching no strings and demanding no privileges." He went on, however, to discuss the benefit to China of economic cooperation by extolling the value of South-South cooperation, which "is of great strategic significance as it helps to break out of the existing international economic relations and create a new international economic order."

Not unnaturally, Beijing is focusing increased media attention on its enlarged aid programs. Despite China's "limited financial and material resources," aid to Third World countries is the PRC's "unshirkable international obligation," according to the Chinese news agency. Beijing's announcement in early 1984 of plans to increase foreign agricultural aid claimed that "China is shouldering responsibility for giving 29 countries 46 kinds of agricultural aid," a generous contribution for a developing country. Most of this agricultural as well as economic aid goes to Africa.

Beijing claims, moreover, to support independent development of Third World national economies "as a sure way to consolidate their political independence," offering itself as a model for such development. An NCNA summary of China's 1983 ties with the Third World claimed "improved economic relations between China and its Third World partners" and said:

> China is still not in a position to provide substantial economic aid. Needless to say, China will continue to provide assistance within its capabilities to those countries confronted with great financial difficulties. Over the last 34 years, China has mastered some advanced experience and technologies which would be helpful to other Third World countries.

China's trade with the Third World is also in the process of transformation. Of particular interest is that the PRC's stress on development of sources of foreign exchange has in recent years transferred some items such as arms and technical services from the area of aid to that of trade. According to the NCNA, the PRC expects to earn at least $1 billion annually in hard currency from its service program by the mid-1980s and by 1985 plans to have 100 thousand technicians under contract in the Third World. The majority of these Chinese, whose services would likely have been donated or provided as part of a low-interest loan package in the 1950s and 1960s, will be persons with rudimentary skills such as those already employed in construction projects in Iraq and in several African countries.

At present, light industrial products represent the bulk of the PRC's exports. Traditionally, such trade has been used as a tool to establish contact with other countries. Although the PRC has a favorable trade balance with much of the Third World, its light industrial products are similar to what other LDCs are producing and thus may not be acceptable. Nor is trade based on light industry capable of supplying the foreign exchange earnings necessary for the PRC to finance a massive modernization program. China is therefore looking elsewhere for lucrative exports and, in addition to labor export, appears to have settled on petroleum and arms sales for which the Third World provides an unlimited market.

The question of arms sales is by far the more complex issue and will most likely involve China in controversy with both superpowers in coming years. Chinese arms sales are up several times over what they were in 1980. Although China cannot compete in the market for sophisticated weaponry, it does produce an extensive line of conventional arms that it is now exporting to the Third World. Already, however, the issue of arms sales confronts China with a critical dilemma in its exercise of interest over principle. Sale of arms to both Iran and Iraq is a policy that runs counter to Beijing's declared policy of promoting a negotiated settlement to the four-year-old controversy between those two nations.[39] The desire for hard cash is probably the overriding factor behind these sales, which are forcefully denied by China because of the public reaction such an admission would risk.

Party-to-Party Ties

There are two other significant levers for achieving influence in the Third World in China's inventory: party-to-party ties — including ties to Communist parties in non-Communist countries — and the use of religion — Islam in particular — as a political tool. Both policies are two-edged swords, which China is learning to employ with increasing caution.

The first, party-to-party ties, reflects China's vision of itself as an international power that will not forsake old friends but is mature enough to establish contacts with ruling political groups having a radically different ideological persuasion. Even though China uses lack of party-to-party ties between the CCP and the Communist Party of the Soviet Union as a tool to express political disagreement, since 1978, Beijing has turned to the establishment of ties with non-Communist political parties as an additional Third World link.

The shift first became evident in February 1979 when Chinese party officials attended the fiftieth anniversary of Mexico's ruling Revolutionary Institutional Party. Then, in April 1979, Beijing announced that it was ready to establish friendly relations with "all Marxist-Leninist parties and all revolutionary political parties fighting for national liberation." The definition has since been expanded to include virtually all parties willing to establish contact with the CCP. Describing development of "friendly relations" with Third World political parties as "a new aspect of our party's international liaison work," and "an important component of our efforts to strengthen unity and cooperation with Third World countries," China now claims to have relations or contacts with some 26 political parties in Latin America alone. Exchange visits by party representatives from all parts of the Third World are frequent.

As a corollary to party ties in the Third World, the PRC has also since the late 1970s sought to expand contact with the European Communist parties and to reestablish relations broken as a result of China's schismatic behavior in the 1960s. Relations have been improved with all East European parties and relations reestablished with the Yugoslav, Greek (KKE), Italian, French, Belgian, and some Scandinavian Communist parties. In Europe, as elsewhere, the PRC no longer supports fringe or divisive "Maoist" groups, a policy of the 1960s that helped blacken China's image in the Third World and failed to result in the establishment of any strong pro-Chinese Communist parties.

A major Chinese press commentary in March 1984 on the importance of party-to-party ties stresses the CCP's support for "the political parties and organizations which are carrying out national liberation struggles, especially those in the Middle East, southern Africa and Central America and the Caribbean region." Failure to mention Asia—or the ongoing Chinese contacts with Communist parties in Indonesia, Burma, and elsewhere in Southeast Asia—highlights the political sensitivity China feels about these ties in view of regional opposition. In an early 1984 statement disclaiming Chinese connections with the Philippine Communist Party, the PRC ambassador said China maintains a policy of noninterference in regard to revolutions because they "are internal affairs."

Religion

In selecting religion as a political tool, Beijing seeks to harness what China correctly believes to be a major factor in Third World politics. The director of Beijing's Religious Affairs Bureau admitted in early 1980 that a major rationale for allowing freedom of religion in China is the widespread influence of Islam in the Third World. Presenting China as a defender of the faith and using China's Muslim population as a credential, the PRC's media portrays the Soviet Union as an enemy of Islam.

China, however, has a population of some 20 to 50 million Muslims, whose capability for disloyalty to the central government has been dramatically displayed several times in this century and the last. Furthermore, Chinese Muslims remain resentful of persecutions and discrimination, particularly during the Cultural Revolution, and the Muslims of Xinjiang are still restive under domination by Han Chinese from the east. The PRC's efforts to arouse Islamic nationalism outside China could backfire—which is perhaps a factor in China's somewhat decreased emphasis on the Islamic factor in Third World politics during 1983 and 1984.

Nonetheless, support for efforts of the Islamic Conference Organization to end the Iran-Iraq war, as well as the PRC's close friendship with Pakistan, have helped to ease China into a cordial relationship with Islamic countries of the Middle East and South Asia. One device used by the PRC has been to identify certain positions that it endorses as Islamic positions – when the audience is Muslim. In particular this has applied to the Afghan resistance to Soviet occupation, which China has at times come close to describing as a holy war.

The dispatch of Muslim delegations was a device used by China in the 1950s to contact Muslim states, and Chinese Muslims making the *hajj* or pilgrimage are still one way China has of contacting Saudi Arabia, which, as an adamantly anti-Communist country, refuses to establish diplomatic relations with the PRC. Efforts to improve relations with Iran following a state visit to Tehran by Premier Hua Guofeng just before the fall of the shah have included Chinese reassurances over the treatment of Muslims in China and religious delegations both sent and received.

Increased use of religious associations under government sponsorship include Chinese religious goodwill delegations to many countries. The Chinese Buddhist Association, the Chinese Islamic Association, the All-China Conference of Protestant Churches, the Chinese Taoist Association, and the Chinese Catholic Patriotic Association – all originally set up in the 1950s – are again in operation. Unfortunately for China's relations with Catholic Third World states, the Chinese Catholic Church was excommunicated in 1957 when, under CCP pressure, it began to elect its own bishops. The Vatican maintains diplomatic relations with Taiwan and, despite contacts between Beijing and the Holy See, no change in China's relationship with the Vatican is expected in the near future.

China's choice of Third World issues as a vehicle for political influence essentially places China in a role of opposition to the existing world order. Yet, unlike the confrontational policy used in the 1960s, Beijing's current policy is to present itself as an elder statesman, a model for development and independence – even as a moral guide to a new, more equitable world order. The advantages of this position are evident in that China, with little risk or expense, receives the Third World's gratitude and portrays itself as the conscience of the developed world.

6

Postscript: Whither China's Quest?

China's post-Cultural Revolution opening to the West has given to the Chinese people a long awaited opportunity to attain international understanding and internal stability. The move toward Third World leadership, an integral part of the PRC's new independent foreign policy is, despite the problems it both encounters and engenders, a healthy sign of a modernizing nation reaching out for a secure international position that will benefit both itself and the rest of the world. The desire for independence but not isolation is, in short, a sign of political maturing.

Despite its rhetoric about independence, the PRC has not rejected the West, as its growing trade and cultural relations demonstrate. But China is feeling its way gingerly in a world it perceives as hostile, not only because of its large aggressive neighbor to the north but also because of its disadvantages in face of Western technological and economic developments. While China goes through its present internal and external policy transformation, the First and Second Worlds would do well to remain sympathetic and supportive but strategically uncommitted — and this is precisely what the PRC wants.

A statement by modern China specialists Liang Heng and Judith Shapiro is as true for China's foreign as for China's domestic direction:

> The more dealings China has with the West and the more stable its economic policies, the greater will be the number of Chinese who have some understanding of western society and are unwilling to return to an emphasis on ideological orthodoxy and class struggle. These people will be China's hope that the two kinds of conservatives, the xenophobic Maoist radicals and those nostalgic for the pro-Soviet 50s, will be unable to muster support for a comeback after Mr. Deng's death.[40]

In this exposure process, the influence of the Third World on China is a positive factor. Since the Cultural Revolution, China has progressively become less defensive internationally, and the CCP's former emphasis on the inevitability of another world war has gradually lessened. This can be attributed in part to a growing Chinese confidence based on its new self-image – for which the Third World is a significant prop. Third World states have in the past several years influenced China to move toward more moderate policies, including less aid and support for Asian Communist parties, a reduced emphasis on the importance of revolutionary armed struggle, an end to the call for precipitous international military action against the Soviet occupation of Afghanistan, and deference to the ASEAN position on the Vietnamese presence in Kampuchea.

The Third World has proven ability to influence the Chinese vote at the UN, not radically or immediately as once hoped, but over a period of time. Chinese support for various Third World issues is of major importance to the developing world because of China's political influence and its position on the UN Security Council. Developing countries can be expected to have a growing impact on China's global posture on such issues as disarmament, nuclear nonproliferation, population control, environmental safeguards, and a variety of other issues. As a corollary, any Chinese tendencies toward restructuring the present international order through radical behavior would likely be braked not only by Third World reservations but by Third World disunity – as well as by the moderating effect that a position of international leadership can be expected to exert on China.

China has not, however, been overwhelmingly successful in its 30-year effort to use the Third World to political advantage. This failure has been due both to China's own misperception and miscalculation and to the changeability, capriciousness, and incapabilities of the Third World nations. Nonetheless, China's failures have been significant. The PRC has not to date played any real role in preventing expansion of either Soviet or U.S. influence. China has no true allies or "satellites," following the post-Cultural Revolution defection of Albania, and it still holds few major positions in international organizations. Perhaps most seriously, its relations with several of the major Third World states are seriously tense (Vietnam and Cuba), strained (India), wary (Angola) or even unofficial (Indonesia and Israel). Nonetheless, past failures have not seriously damaged China's potential for increasing its Third World authority, and, for the first time, with a policy of independence and with a moderate leadership, China appears in a good position to do so.

The strength of China's position as a contender for a significant leadership role in the Third World should not be underestimated by the developed world. Despite Third World factionalism, which complicates Chinese efforts to forge a unified front of developed states, China's unique global position is sufficient to attract considerable Third World attention and respect. One need only reflect that there is no Soviet-U.S.-Bolivian triangle or even a Soviet-U.S.-Indian triangle in the sense in which there is a Soviet-U.S.-China triangular relationship.

Not only is China the only permanent Third World member of the Security Council, it is a member of the nuclear club and, in April 1984, demonstrated its growing technological capability by launching its first permanent orbiting communications satellite. China's space program contributes to the PRC's Third World mystique – as does Beijing's independent stance on issues such as nuclear control and laws governing chemical warfare. The Third World, whatever reservations some members may have, is proud of a developing state that can flaunt the superpowers.

The significance of China's position as a participant in both the East-West strategic and North-South economic balance of power is not approached by either India or Japan. And the fact that China treats itself as a great power is not without significance in arousing a similar assessment in the Third World. Third World appreciation for China's interest in its economic development and political independence adds luster to China's international position. China scholar Samuel Kim warns against allowing the Chinese practice of linking the economic demands of the Third World to "imperialist" practices of the superpowers to distract attention from "the many positive aspects of Chinese support for the global underdogs."[41]

The weaknesses in China's aspirations to power also remain evident. Factors inhibiting China's drive for leadership include Third World recognition that the Chinese effort to adopt an independent policy is in itself an admission of dependence and thus of weakness. In other words, if China were truly strong enough to be independent, Beijing would not have to insist on the point. The PRC's Third World policy sometimes seems formulated only to increase favor in the Third World or to demonstrate China's Third World identity by embarrassing the superpowers or hindering their influence. This sort of reactive Chinese policy – such as China's UN voting record on disarmament and its rhetoric against U.S. policy in Central America and southern Africa – has in the past been an irritant to some Third World states, which see China's scoldings of the superpowers as unnecessarily confrontational.

Harry Harding points out that, although the Chinese have made good use of their limited resources in building influence in the Third World, they have been considerably less successful in selecting issues around which to rally Third World support.[42] The PRC has, moreover, a long way to go toward understanding the Third World and successfully managing its relations there. Both isolation and a Sinocentric world view have contributed to China's lack of knowledge or, even at times, interest in Third World countries beyond a surface level. The PRC's view of the developing world is still too simple, too prone to ignore Third World divisions and internal difficulties, too ready to paint a world of black and white in which blame accrues to the superpowers alone.

Other problems the PRC faces in building its Third World position are financial and historical. Financial resources, no matter how carefully managed, still restrict China's ability to compete with the developed world through major aid programs and also puts China into direct competition with other Third World states for development funding. Historical problems include China's lack of diplomatic expertise, its peoples' scant exposure to foreign languages and cultures, and its lack of experience in leadership roles in international organizations.

Image problems are an even more difficult problem and stem not only from the Cultural Revolution's era of belligerence but also from Asian Third World fears of Chinese aggressiveness as a result of Chinese policies toward Hong Kong, Taiwan, Tibet, and Vietnam. Finally, China's size, its seat on the Security Council, and its nuclear capabilities raise fears in some Third World circles that the PRC is not really a Third World state, but a superpower, whose needs are not compatable with the Third World over the long term.

To question how real is the independence of China's foreign policy raises a second question: how much influence has China as the minor partner in the Sino-Soviet-U.S. triangle? An increase of tensions between the United States and the Soviet Union during 1983 was not related to China nor does Beijing have much scope for manipulation of the Washington-Moscow relationship. Furthermore, U.S. reiteration beginning in 1982 of the centrality of Japan in Asia's defense and for U.S. policy in Asia may mean a more mature recognition by all parties of the limits of China's influence as a Pacific power. One of the benefits to the United States of the post-1982 Chinese policy is, in fact, a more realistic U.S. view of the realities of the Sino-U.S. relationship – including the demise of the unrealistic hope that the PRC would support U.S. initiatives in the Third World, particularly with reference to the USSR.

Nonetheless, China's assets considerably outweigh its liabilities in the Third World ledger, and Beijing can expect to play an increasingly important role in Third World politics in years ahead. A significant degree of Third World economic cooperation under China's leadership or a Chinese decision to play a major role in international arms negotiations could provide valuable avenues of influence for the Third World. Over the long term, a Chinese Third World leadership role would appear to be almost inevitable. This will be as true for China's role as moral adviser as for China's ability to muster support for issues of relevance to the Third World.

Third World nations reject large amounts of China's rhetoric and even resent the disparity between that rhetoric and actual Chinese practice – for example, China's failure to support some legitimate revolutionary movements while maintaining close ties with governments run by military dictatorships. There is also a high degree of awareness in the Third

World that China's foreign policy is much more pragmatic than ideological and that the Three Worlds theory and the Five Principles of Mutual Coexistence are at heart convenient tools to advance China's position. In reality the PRC has built a system of foreign relations that allows China to strengthen ties with capitalist dictatorships such as Chile and Communist revisionists such as Yugoslavia, while simultaneously carrying on a bitter controversy with Marxist states such as Cuba, Vietnam, and Afghanistan – all Third World countries but all closely tied to the USSR. But, by and large, the developing world admires China's ability to balance all these relationships. The Third World regards China as an increasingly successful Third World state to whom the superpowers will listen, and, perhaps equally important, one sincerely seeking to better the Third World's economic leverage.

China's main routes to leadership in the Third World are through Chinese authority in Third World organizations, either by membership or the good offices of friends, and through consolidation by China of its Asian leadership role. Both avenues have many pitfalls, and China will move slowly. But if China can achieve a position of greater political independence from the superpowers based on strong Third World ties, a less defensive and more stable and globally responsible China is likely to be the result.

Notes

1. Peter Van Ness, *Revolution and Chinese Foreign Policy: Peking's Support for Wars of National Liberation* (Los Angeles, Calif.: University of California Press, 1970), 15.

2. *Beijing Review*, August 9, 1982.

3. See *People's Daily* editorial in *Beijing Review*, November 4, 1977. Since adoption as official Chinese policy in 1974, the Three Worlds theory has gone through several permutations. For a brief period between the 1979 establishment of diplomatic relations with the United States and the Soviet invasion of Afghanistan approximately one year later, China promoted U.S. leadership in a worldwide "united front" defense against what it saw as an expanded threat from the Soviet Union. Chinese leaders said little about the Three Worlds theory during that period, and Western analysts began to wonder if China might not be in the process of permanently revising the concept.

4. Ishwer C. Ojha, *Chinese Foreign Policy in an Age of Transition: The Diplomacy of Cultural Despair* (Boston, Mass.: Beacon Press, 1969), xi–xii.

5. Since the 1950s, China's foreign aid has characteristically been given to labor intensive but relatively inexpensive projects such as factories, roads, and port facilities, which come quickly into operation, are highly visible, and bring immediate benefit to local people.

6. China claims it has only 14 million Muslims, but various Western authorities put the number between 20 and 50 million.

7. Ojha, *Chinese Foreign Policy*, 200.

8. China did not publicly call for a U.S.-led anti-Soviet united front until after the Soviet invasion of Afghanistan. But the concept itself was there in less explicit fashion as early as 1970 when the official military journal, *Red Flag*, justified the idea of a Sino-U.S. détente in united front terms. The concept of a U.S.-led united front became further evident in the mid-1970s after Moscow had become China's foremost international enemy.

9. Lin Piao's six points for People's War were (1) a broad united front of all classes; (2) the leading role of the party; (3) establishment of base areas; (4) an army founded on mass support and aided by a peasantry loyal to both the party and the army; (5) correct military tactics, i.e. guerrilla warfare; and (6) self-reliance.

10. I am particularly grateful to Dr. Carol Lee Hamrin of the U.S. Department of State, whose careful research and analysis, particularly on China's internal political developments, have influenced my analysis.

11. UN Document A/32/PV, 3, September 29, 1977, p. 56.

12. Bruce D. Larkin, "China and the Third World in Global Perspective," in James C. Hsiung and Samuel S. Kim, eds., *China in the Global Community* (New York: Praeger, 1980), 64.

13. Ojha, *Chinese Foreign Policy*, 181.

14. Shao, Kuo-kang, "Chou En-lai's Diplomatic Approach to Non-Aligned States in Asia: 1953–60," *China Quarterly*, no. 78 (June 1979): 324.

15. China has been vague about the origins of the Five Principles of Peaceful Coexistence, sometimes claiming Zhou's sole authorship and sometimes sharing credit with India and Burma. The Five Principles are (1) mutual respect for sovereignty and territorial integrity, (2) mutual nonaggression, (3) noninterference in each other's internal affairs, (4) equality and mutual benefit, and (5) peaceful coexistence. Beijing has retained verbal adherence to these principles, referring to them frequently in its media and incorporating them into the PRC Constitutions of 1978 and 1982.

16. Charles Neuhauser, *Third World Politics: China and the Afro-Asian People's Solidarity Organization 1957–1967* (Cambridge,

Mass.: East Asia Research Center, Harvard University Press, 1968), 70.

17. Frederick C. Teiwes, "Chinese Politics 1949–65: A Changing Mao," Part I, *Current Scene* 12, no. 1 (January 1974): 6.

18. "Mao's Talk with Anna Louise Strong, August 1946," *Selected Works* 4 (Beijing: Foreign Languages Press, 1969): 97–101.

19. Robert C. North, *The Foreign Relations of China*, 3rd ed. (North Scituate, Mass.: Duxbury Press, 1978), 99.

20. Neuhauser, *Third World Politics*, 62.

21. Robert L. Worden, "China's Foreign Relations in Latin America," in C. T. Hsueh, ed., *Dimensions of China's Foreign Relations* (New York: Praeger, 1977), 196.

22. Conscious of its lack of an international institutional position, the PRC had publicly discussed the possibility of organizing a rival UN organization centered on Indonesia. This possibility came to naught with the 1965 Indonesian coup.

23. Diplomatic ties were established between the PRC and Pakistan in 1951, but the friendship did not flower until their perception of mutual interests came about in the early 1960s.

24. George T. Yu, "China's Failure in Africa," *Asian Survey* 6, no. 8 (August 1966): 468.

25. Van Ness, *Revolution*, 82ff.

26. Chalmers Johnson, *Autopsy on People's War* (Berkeley, Calif.: University of California Press, 1973), 13.

27. Although the ninth party congress marked the termination of the most violent stage of the Cultural Revolution, China now claims that the Great Proletariat Cultural Revolution era actually lasted for ten years: from 1966 until the death of Mao in 1976.

28. Carol Lee Hamrin, "Competing 'Policy Packages' in Post-Mao China," *Asian Survey* 24, no. 5 (May 1984): 489.

29. Ibid., 488.

30. China has signed no formal alliances with any states other than the 1961 friendship and security treaty with the People's Democratic Republic of Korea and the 1950 treaty with the USSR. (Pyongyang has a virtually identical treaty with Moscow, which also dates from 1961.) China's inability to "control" North Korea is clearly of concern in light of the responsibilities outlined for Korean defense under this treaty.

31. *Beijing Review* declared in April 1984 that despite "shifts" in U.S. Asia-Pacific policy, "it is nonetheless clear that in view of global strategic needs, Washington will have to get involved in the Pacific rim." In Foreign Broadcast Information Service (FBIS), "Daily Reports: China," April 25, 1984, B-5.

32. Until recently China officially prohibited trade, direct or indirect, with South Korea, Israel, and South Africa. Unofficially, however, limited amounts of commercial contact have existed between China and all three countries for several years.

33. William Branigan, "Border Calm Despite War Talk," *Washington Post*, April 30, 1984.

34. Elsewhere in the Third World a similar flexibility toward Soviet clients has been evident in China's establishment of diplomatic ties with Angola in 1982 and present moves to gain a closer relationship with Nicaragua.

35. Michael Weisskopf, "China Calls Invasion 'Bloody Aggression,'" *Washington Post*, November 6, 1983.

36. Proposals for "nuclear free zones" and "zones of peace" are inevitably in the Third World, but do not always overlap. For example, India, a nuclear state, proposes the Indian Ocean as a zone of peace; in 1973 the PRC signed Protocol II of the Treaty of Tlatelolco (Treaty for the Prohibition of Nuclear Weapons in Latin America), which would guarantee Latin America as a nuclear free zone, and China recently reiterated support for Nepal's 1975 declaration of itself as a zone of peace, a prudent posture for a small state located between two large nuclear neighbors.

37. Issues such as the shooting down of the South Korean airliner, which found the Third World divided, present China with hard choices. But the PRC is not a pushover for Third World pressures where it feels other principles must be applied. China has, for example, continued a close relationship with Chile's leader Augusto Pinochet, despite considerable Third World criticism, seeing the relationship as economically and strategically beneficial, and has refused to join Third World sponsored resolutions at the UN condemning the Pinochet regime's violations of human rights.

38. The height of the PRC's foreign aid program – including the crest of Chinese aid to revolutionary groups – came during the 1960s. China's "Eight Principles of Foreign Aid," as proclaimed by Premier Zhou in 1964, stipulated (1) equality and mutual benefit,

(2) respect for the other country's sovereignty, (3) interest free or low interest loans with flexible repayment schedules, (4) self-reliance and independent economic development, (5) projects requiring low investment and producing quick results, (6) provision of quality Chinese equipment and manufactured goods, (7) training of indigenous technicians, and (8) adherence by Chinese experts and advisers to the living standard of their counterparts in the recipient country.

39. See for example, "China Secretly Selling Arms to Iran," *Washington Post*, April 3, 1984. China has denied these reports.

40. Liang Heng and Judith Shapiro, "Reagan in China: Effect-I," *New York Times*, April 22, 1984.

41. Samuel S. Kim, "Chinese Global Policy: An Assessment," in Hsiung and Kim, *China in the Global Community*, 223.

42. Harry Harding, "China and the Third World: From Revolution to Containment," in Richard H. Solomon, ed., *The China Factor* (Englewood Cliffs, N.J.: Prentice-Hall, 1981), 283.

Appendix
China's Diplomatic Relations

A. *Countries Having Diplomatic Relations With the People's Republic of China* (date of the establishment of relations in parentheses)

Afghanistan (January 1955)
Albania (November 1949)
Algeria (September 1958, with Provisional Government)
Angola (January 1983)
Argentina (February 1972)
Australia (December 1972)
Austria (May 1971)
Bangladesh (October 1975)
Barbados (May 1977)
Belgium (October 1971)
Benin (resumed December 1972)
Botswana (January 1975)
Brazil (August 1974)
Bulgaria (October 1949)

Burma (December 1949)
Burundi (resumed October 1971)
Cambodia (July 1958)
Cameroon (March 1971)
Canada (October 1970)
Cape Verde Islands (April 1976)
Central African Republic (resumed August 1976)
Chad (November 1972)
Chile (December 1970)
Colombia (February 1980)
Comoro Islands (November 1975)
Congo (Brazzaville) (February 1964)

Cuba (September 1960)
Cyprus (January 1972)
Czechoslovakia (October 1949)
Denmark (May 1950)
Djibouti (January 1979)
Ecuador (January 1980)
Egypt (May 1956)
Equatorial Guinea (October 1970)
Ethiopia (November 1970)
Fiji Islands (November 1975)
Finland (October 1950)
France (January 1964)
Gabon (April 1974)
Gambia (December 1974)
Germany, East – German Democratic Republic (October 1949)
Germany, West – Federal Republic of Germany (recognized October 1950 but relations not established until October 1972)
Ghana (resumed February 1972)
Greece (June 1972)
Guinea (October 1959)
Guinea-Bissau (March 1974)
Guyana (June 1972)
Hungary (October 1949)
Iceland (December 1971)
India (April 1950)

Iran (August 1971)
Iraq (August 1958)
Ireland (June 1979)
Italy (November 1970)
Ivory Coast (March 1983)
Jamaica (November 1972)
Japan (September 1972)
Jordan (April 1977)
Kenya (December 1963)
Kiribati (June 1980)
Korea, North – Democratic People's Republic of Korea (October 1949)
Kuwait (March 1971)
Laos (September 1962)
Lebanon (November 1971)
Lesotho (May 1983)
Liberia (February 1977)
Libya (August 1978)*
Luxembourg (November 1972)
Madagascar (November 1972)
Malaysia (May 1974)
Maldives (October 1972)
Mali (October 1960)
Malta (January 1972)
Mauritania (July 1965)
Mauritius (April 1972)
Mexico (February 1972)
Mongolia (October 1949)
Morocco (November 1958)
Mozambique (June 1975)
Nepal (August 1955)

---

*Libya unilaterally announced recognition of the PRC in 1971, but owing to the presence in Tripoli of an ambassador from Taiwan, formal PRC-Libyan relations were not established until 1978.

Netherlands (November 1954)
New Zealand (December 1972)
Niger (July 1974)
Nigeria (February 1971)
Norway (October 1954)
Oman (May 1978)
Pakistan (May 1951)
Papua New Guinea (October 1976)
Peru (November 1971)
Philippines (June 1975)
Poland (October 1949)
Portugal (February 1979)
Romania (October 1949)
Rwanda (November 1971)
San Marino (May 1971, consular only)
Sao Tome and Principe (July 1975)
Senegal (December 1971)
Seychelles Islands (June 1976)
Sierra Leone (July 1971)
Somalia (December 1960)
Spain (March 1973)
Sri Lanka (February 1957)
Sudan (December 1958)
Surinam (May 1976)
Sweden (May 1959)
Switzerland (September 1950)

Syria (August 1956)
Tanzania (October 1964)
Thailand (July 1975)
Togo (September 1972)
Trinidad and Tobago (June 1974)
Tunisia (resumed October 1971)
Turkey (August 1971)
Uganda (October 1962)
United Arab Emirates (November 1984)
United Kingdom (June 1954)
United States (January 1979)
USSR (October 1949)
Upper Volta (September 1973)
Vanuatu (March 1982)
Venezuela (June 1974)
Vietnam (January 1950)*
Western Samoa (November 1975)
Yemen, North – Yemen Arab Republic (August 1956)
Yemen, South – People's Democratic Republic of Yemen (February 1968)
Yugoslavia (January 1955)
Zaire (November 1972)
Zambia (October 1964)

---

*Prior to the formation of the Socialist Republic of Vietnam (July 1976), the PRC had separate relations with North Vietnam (January 1950) and the Provisional Revolutionary Government of South Vietnam (June 1969).

B. Countries That Recognize, But Have No Official Relations With, the People's Republic of China

Bhutan – October 1971 (Recognition is based on the UN vote to admit the PRC and expel representatives of Taipei.)

Indonesia – April 1950 (PRC relations with Indonesia were ruptured in 1965 following Jakarta's accusation of Beijing's implication in a coup attempt.)

Israel – January 1950 (Israel has not been recognized by the PRC.)

C. Countries Maintaining Diplomatic Relations With Taipei (Date of the establishment of recent relations in parentheses.)

Bolivia	Panama
Costa Rica	Paraguay
Dominican Republic	St. Christopher and Nevis
Dominica (May 1983)	(October 1983)
El Salvador	St. Lucia (January 1984)
Guatemala	St. Vincent and the
Haiti	Grenadines (August 1981)
Holy See	Saudi Arabia
Honduras	Solomon Islands (March 1983)
Korea, South (Republic of Korea)	South Africa
Malawi	Swaziland
Nauru	Tonga
Nicaragua	Tuvalu
	Uruguay

D. Countries That Neither Recognize Nor Have Official Relations With the People's Republic of China or Taipei

Bahamas	Grenada
Bahrain*	Qatar
Belize	Singapore*

/

---

*Singapore and Bahrain have permitted Taiwan to establish trade missions that also handle consular matters. These states do not consider this as recognition and have no missions in Taiwan.

Authoritative Interpretations of International Events...

THE UNITED NATIONS
Reality and Ideal
Peter R. Baehr and **Leon Gordenker**
Take a close look at the U.N. with this straightforward account of its work over the past 40 years. The authors discuss the organization's effectiveness and efficiency and offer suggestions for improvement.

| 224 pp. | July 1984 | ISBN 0-03-062757-5 | $28.95 |

TURKEY
The Politics of Authority, Democracy, and Development
Frank Tachau
A detailed discussion of constitutional changes... economic development... sociocultural changes... foreign affairs in Turkey over the past 30 years.

| ca. 178 pp. | August 1984 | ISBN 0-03-052626-4 | ca. $27.95 |

THE SINO-VIETNAMESE CONFLICT
Eugene K. Lawson
"...a sobering revision of many of the accepted conclusions which determined America's policy.... his fine work will help us see facets of that experience we did not appreciate at the time."—William Colby

| 336 pp. | August 1984 | ISBN 0-03-070733-1 | $ 27.95 |

ROMANIAN FOREIGN POLICY AND THE UNITED NATIONS
Also of interest... **Robert Weiner**

| | 218 pp. | July 1984 | ISBN 0-03-071594-6 | $29.95 |

THE EMERGENCE OF A NEW LEBANON   Fantasy or Reality?
Edward E. Azar, Paul A. Jureidini, R.D. McLaurin, Augustus R. Norton, Robert J. Pranger, Kate Shnayerson, Lewis W. Snider, and **Joyce R. Starr**

| ca. 256 pp. | October 1984 | ISBN 0-03-070736-6 | ca. $25.95 |

Available through your local bookseller or order directly from:
PRAEGER PUBLISHERS
521 Fifth Avenue, New York, New York 10175

WHAT'S NEXT FOR THE WORLD'S DEVELOPED ECONOMIES?

BEYOND INDUSTRIALIZATION
Ascendancy of the Global Service Economy

Ronald Kent Shelp, Vice President.
International Relations, American International Group, Inc.

"Ron Shelp has developed an impressive analysis of trade in services, likely to become a major reference work for trade negotiators in the years ahead. Services is on the cutting edge of trade negotiations in the 80's, and this volume sharply delineates the problems—and opportunities—of services trade."
—William Brock, U.S. Trade Representative

"Ron Shelp dramatizes the results of our repeated failure to recognize the implications of being a service economy. He describes how our domestic and foreign economic policies are formed without taking into account this reality. His conclusion should be heeded: We will fail to achieve economic growth and price stability, and fail to be a successful competitor in world markets unless we fit services into our policy framework. Mr. Shelp's analysis and history of past OECD and GATT discussions and negotiations (with the litany of protectionist rationale) is most enlightening and a necessary prelude for anyone now turning to this topic."
—Senator Daniel Patrick Moynihan

"It is rare that a business executive takes time to produce a seminal work that addresses a broad range of important policy questions that will be grappled with for the rest of this century."
**—David M. Abshire, Chairman,
Georgetown University's Center for Strategic
and International Studies**

"Mr. Shelp documents the rise of the global service economy and lays the groundwork for the coming negotiation to liberalize services trade."
**—Robert S. Strauss,
former U.S. Trade Representative**

"The U.S. Government and American business are pushing for international agreements to liberalize the trade in services. This pioneering book by one of the leading participants in the process helps explain why and gives the first extensive account of past efforts...the book breaks new ground and should stimulate further discussion."
—Foreign Affairs

"...one of the basic reference works in the field."
—Clyde H. Farnsworth, New York Times

Indicates that there are some legitimate and troublesome questions relating to the evolution of the most advanced nations into service economies. Although it's generally recognized among policymakers that the most advanced economies are service economies, the author points out that this fact is not translated into government policy. For example, when faced with inflation, officials focus on structural defects of the manufacturing sector, such as large wage settlements, but they don't come to grips with service industry induced inflation. The author maintains that policy makers overlook the significant role of services in the international economy. In this study he examines the role of services in the industrialized, developing and socialist economies. He reviews the regulations of services in international commerce and proposes steps to liberalize the flow of services internationally.
256 pp.   1982 $29.95
ISBN 0-03-059304-2

Available through your local bookseller, or order directly from:

PRAEGER
P U B L I S H E R S
521 Fifth Avenue, New York, N.Y. 10175

THE FEDERAL RESERVE, MONEY, AND INTEREST RATES

The Volcker Years and Beyond
Michael G. Hadjimichalakis

Analyzes the contemporary operations and goals of the Federal Reserve and examines analytically and factually the record of the Volcker years. Explains the errors that led to the 1981–82 recession of the emergence of the new financial environment of (financial) deregulation.

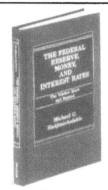

| 288 pp. | June 1984 | $29.95 | ISBN 0-03-063861-5 |

NEW DIRECTIONS IN ECONOMIC POLICY

An Agenda for the 1980s
Everett M. Ehrlich and **Raymond C. Scheppach**

Here is a lively new book on domestic economic policy which defines and analyzes the major economic issues facing America during the decade of the '80s.

| 224 pp. | June 1984 | $27.95 | ISBN 0-03-063786-4 |

U.S. WOOD-BASED INDUSTRY

Industrial Organization and Performance
Paul V. Ellefson and **Robert N. Stone**

| ca. 320 pp. | September 1984 | ca. $25.95 | ISBN 0-03-063698-1 |

GREECE AND YUGOSLAVIA

An Economic Comparison
Nicholas V. Gianaris

| 272 pp. | June 1984 | $34.95 | ISBN 0-03-071466-4 |

INDUSTRIAL RELATIONS IN LATIN AMERICA

edited by **Efren Cordova**

| 288 pp. | March 1984 | $28.95 | ISBN 0-03-070284-4 |

Available through your local bookseller, or order directly from:

PRAEGER PUBLISHERS 521 Fifth Avenue New York, N.Y. 10175

www.ingramcontent.com/pod-product-compliance
Ingram Content Group UK Ltd.
Pitfield, Milton Keynes, MK11 3LW, UK
UKHW020736280225
455688UK00012B/695